**Losses in Later Life
A New Way of Walking with God**

ntegration Books

STUDIES IN PASTORAL PSYCHOLOGY,
THEOLOGY, AND SPIRITUALITY

Robert J. Wicks,
General Editor

also in this series

Clinical Handbook of Pastoral Counseling
R. Wicks, R. Parsons, and D. Capps (Eds.)

*Adolescents in Turmoil,
Parents Under Stress*
Richard D. Parsons

Pastoral Marital Therapy
Stephen Treat and Larry Hof

The Art of Clinical Supervision
B. Estadt, J. Compton and M. Blanchette (Eds.)

The Art of Passingover
Francis Dorff

Losses in Later Life

A New Way of
Walking with God

R. Scott Sullender, Ph.D.

Integration Books

paulist press/new york and mahwah

Library of Congress Cataloging-in-Publication Data

Sullender, R. Scott.
    Losses in later life: a new way of walking with God/by R. Scott
    Sullender.
    p.   cm.—(Integration books)
    Bibliography: p.
    ISBN 0-8091-3034-3 (pbk.) : $8.95
    1. Loss (Psychology) in old age.   2. Life change events in old
age—Psychological aspects.   3. Adjustment (Psychology) in old age.
4. Aging—Psychological aspects.   5. Aged—Psychology.   6. Aged—
Religious life.   I. Title.   II. Series.
BF724.85.L67S85 1989
155.6—dc19   88-25438
                                                                  CIP

Published by Paulist Press
997 Macarthur Boulevard
Mahwah, N.J. 07430

Printed and bound in the
United States of America

Contents

Dedicated to
Robert Thomas Sullender
1921—1985

Foreword

Change is inevitable. Losses are natural. And, no matter how drastic one's denial may be regarding these two facts of life, the events of later adulthood force one to eventually face them.

In *Losses in Later Life,* Scott Sullender discusses the major and unique aspects of such losses at this dynamic period of life. The information he provides reflects the multifaceted nature of different losses in the second half of life in such a sensitive, practical and clear manner, that both those in ministry and persons within this age group would benefit from reading this book.

Meeting the challenges of the later years requires a willingness to accept the value of being the age we are—no matter whether that age is viewed by some as "old" and "unattractive" or is seen as a time of "wisdom" and "graciousness." The call of later life, as Sullender well demonstrates, is to develop "a new way of walking with God" by avoiding the temptation to make idols out of the past and to grieve the losses that are now coming upon us with increased rapidity. This grieving process is essential if we hope to find the new identities and spiritual meanings that are hidden from us earlier in our life span.

Losses in later life can lead to gains. But we must have not only the right attitude, but also helpful information on how to use the realities that later life presents for gain rather than disillusionment and bitterness. Sullender in this work helps us to help ourselves and others with respect to this stage. He aids us to be "good grievers" and to seek the spiritual and psychological possibilities that are often present when we can let go of our resistances and preconceived notions of what it means to be an older adult. This work is full of information on the varied losses of later life (e.g. youth, family, parents, work, spouse, health, and identity). Sullender has done a real service in his preparation of *Losses in Later Life*. I recommend it to you most highly. It will be quite useful to you both in your ministry and in your personal life.

Robert J. Wicks
Series Editor

Introduction

Life is a journey. There are many stages along the way. Most of these stages include loss experiences. We lose people we love, through death, through divorce, through "growing apart." We can lose a job, a home, a pet or a valued possession. We can also lose moments, ideals, dreams and health. Some losses are sudden and very painful. Others come upon us more gradually and with mixed feelings. Either way losses are inevitable. They seem to be part and parcel of the nature of life itself. The terrible agony of an unwanted loss is as "natural" to life as is the joy of new birth, and in some cases they are mysteriously linked.

The losses that occur during the first half of life are often couched in terms of growth and development. Losing our first tooth, graduating from school and losing one's innocence are often understood as prerequisites for growth. These are necessary losses. These losses are celebrated as much as they are mourned. People do experience accidental losses during the first half of life, but generally these are the exceptions to the rule. The vast majority of losses in early life are developmental in nature.

As we pass over into the second half of life, however, losses take on a different character. The losses that we now experience are more frequent, more permanent and more negative in nature. They are no longer couched as "growth experiences" (although they can be) nor are they always celebrated. Losses also begin to become cumulative in nature after age forty. Losses build upon losses. Each loss is linked to previous losses, and in a sense foreshadows the ultimate loss of life itself. The losses of later life are essentially different in character from the losses of the first half of life. Therefore, we need to understand in particular the losses of the second half of life and how to deal with them in ways that augment our emotional and spiritual health. This is the task of this book.

Before we turn our attention to a discussion of these losses per se, however, we will discuss the nature of grief and the nature of spiritual health. The chapter on grief dynamics is a somewhat brief summary of the nature of grief. For a fuller discussion of this important topic, I refer you to my earlier book, *Grief and Growth: Pastoral Resources for Emotional and Spiritual Growth*, by this same publisher. A solid understanding of the nature of grief, along with a perspective on spiritual health, is foundational to our task of forging an "integrated" approach to understanding loss in later life. It is to these subjects that we turn initially, followed by chapters on what I consider to be the key losses of later life. In conclusion, the last chapter will take a wider look at loss and aging from the vantage point of faith.

In this book I have focused on seven major losses: loss of youth, loss of family, loss of parents, loss of work, loss of spouse, loss of health and loss of identity. There are shorter discussions on several additional losses which have been placed in the chapter where they seem best to fit. However, each person's journey is unique. Some readers may find one of these major losses to be relatively "minor" in their lives. Others may find that a loss that I have given minor attention to has been quite "major" in their experience. I think however that most of us will pass through each of the losses discussed in this book in some form or another.

I would also like to note that I have not placed these losses in any specific chronological order, although some people will argue for such. Each loss is as much a process that colors all of the years of later life as it is a single event. In fact I would argue that each loss is experienced both as event and as process. That is part of the nature of loss in the later years.

My gratitude goes to the people who have read all or portions of this manuscript and given me helpful feedback. I appreciate your support. I would also like to thank my colleagues and friends at the Walnut Valley Counseling Center, who put up with my absence while I was writing this book. Most importantly, I am grateful for the many people who have shared their losses with me, as their pastor, friend and counselor. Many of their stories, appropriately disguised, are included in this book in the hopes that their experience will enrich all of us. May God bless your reading and your journey.

R. Scott Sullender
Claremont, California

Chapter 1

The Grief Dynamic

" . . . and you will know the truth and the truth will set you free" (Jn 8:32).

Grief is, simply put, that human emotion that we feel when we lose someone or something that we are psychologically attached to. It is the feeling of sorrow, sadness and nostalgia. It occurs every time there is a loss. Grief is therefore universal among humans. Yet grief feelings can vary widely in intensity depending on how emotionally attached we were to that which is lost. Obviously when we lose someone very important to us, we grieve with intensity, very long and very deeply. If, however, we lose something less important psychologically to us or something that we have partially accepted as already lost, then our experience of grief is light, subtle and short-lived. In some of the latter cases we might not notice that we are grieving at all.

Grief's Pain and Its Defenses

Grief is painful. That sounds like an obvious statement. Yet, it needs to be emphasized. Grief feelings are painful feelings. The pain may be intense or light, but it is pain. Unlike physical pain, the pain of grief is not something one can readily see or easily soothe with cold compresses or carefully prescribed medications. Grief is essentially a subjective experience, which is largely in the mind, or, shall I say, in the heart of the griever. To the sorrower the pain of grief is very real and it is as powerful and as influential in his/life as any physical ailment could be.

Most humans do not like pain as such and seek to avoid it whenever possible. So too, most of us go to lengths to avoid the pain of grief as well. When we see a loss coming down the road of life, we tend to pretend that it won't happen to us or that it's still too far away to worry about. When we are told that a loss is about to happen, we tend to look for ways to prevent it or to escape its consequences. And when a loss has occurred, we are slow to fully realize that the loss is final, irreversible and demanding of adjustments in our lives. It is little wonder then that most people have difficulty with grief. Indeed, it has been my experience that most modern Americans have great trouble handling grief feelings. Our efforts to deny it, avoid it or defer its full impact hamper our ability to be healed in a timely and easy manner.

These mental "tricks" that we play on ourselves, to avoid, deny or soften the impact of grief's pain, are what psychologists call "defense mechanisms." A defense mechanism is any mental mechanism used by us to shield us from pain, in this case, psychological pain. Defense mechanisms are not all bad. In fact, they are quite necessary. We could not cope with pain without some means to moderate its intensity. Yet a prolonged clinging to defense mechanisms, in the face of a reality that demands the opposite, can lead to serious mental, emotional and familial problems.

In the context of bereavement, there can be many types of defense mechanisms. There are, however, certain common ones.

Denial: Denial is the psychological mechanism whereby we avoid emotionally realizing that the loss has occurred or is about to occur. We deny its reality. We literally pretend it's not there. Denial comes in varying forms and degrees.[1] A first degree denial, the most serious kind, occurs when a person totally denies the reality of an imminent loss and even denies all of the related facts surrounding its existence. A woman who has a terminal illness, for example, may deny that she has any illness at all or has even been to the hospital recently. This is the extreme! But the pain of the imminent loss of life is so intense, so devastating that she must deny, at least for the moment, all facts related to the situation. She will literally blot it out from her mind.

Another person (or the same person at a later stage of bereavement) may admit cognitively and verbally that the loss has occurred, but emotionally he/she still feels as if it hasn't really happened. This is called a second degree denial. Dr. Mortimer characterizes this type of denial as "It happened, but who cares?" The individual acknowledges the loss, but is emotionally turned off or anesthetized.[2] A grieving wife might say, "I know that he is gone, but I just cannot accept it. It feels like he's still here, like he's out there, on a business trip and will be driving back into the driveway any time now." This type of denial is not as extreme as a first degree denial and usually leads, in time, to a full realization of the loss. It is as if this woman's emotions need time to catch up with what her mind already knows. Emotions change slower than cognitions.

Yet a third person (or the same person at a still later stage of bereavement) may admit the reality of the loss cognitively and may even have emotionally worked it through, but he/she still has not fully adjusted to the loss and continues to act as if life is the same as it was prior to the loss. This is called a third degree denial. This is the mildest type of denial. People can be slow to make adjustments to their new status or identity. The unemployed man delays seeking a new job. The grieving husband is slow to get rid of his wife's sewing machine or her favorite dresses. The handicapped woman continues to try to do it on her own. Behavior then is the final and slowest piece of our lives to accept the full reality of a loss. We can still deny a loss behaviorally long after we have come to accept it, cognitively and emotionally.

Viewed from this perspective, the process of grieving could be understood as a passing through different levels of denial. At each stage the griever accepts a little more of the full reality of the loss, until finally he/she embraces the loss with his whole being. If the loss comes as an unexpected, unwanted tragedy, we may begin with a first stage denial. We are shocked, numbed by the pain. Gradually, though, we accept the loss cognitively. We know it happened. Then we come to feel it, at first marginally and then deeply. We work it through emotionally. Finally, our behavior catches up with the process and we make the necessary changes that the loss requires. Now we live it.

Generally speaking, denial is a costly defense mechanism. In order to pretend that something didn't happen, we must distort the truth so badly that this distortion itself causes us great psychological harm. In addition denial requires great psychic energy to maintain, energies that could be spent living. Denial II, denying our emotions, is also very costly. It seems to be a truism that if we repress one emo-

tion, we inevitably repress them all. People who cannot or who re-
fuse to grieve are often people who also cannot love. There is little
joy, little love, little anger . . . little anything emotionally. They are
dead people. Yet, I have found that when these persons start grieving again, they experience a flood of emotions of all kinds. Suddenly
they are able to feel again—feel anger, feel love, feel joy . . . feel
alive.

Rationalization: Rationalization is a defense mechanism
whereby we offer explanations for why a loss really isn't so bad. We
rationalize the loss, so that the pain does not hurt quite so bad. We
make excuses to and for ourselves. Rationalization is largely a cognitive process. It is a way of comforting ourselves. Rationalizations
ease our pain. If we have lost a job, we say, "It really wasn't such a
good job after all. The boss was a grouch and the pay was lousy." If
we have lost our home, we might say, "I didn't like that neighborhood anyhow. Those teenagers were always so noisy and unruly. We
will find a better place to live." If we have lost a parent in death, we
may say, "Well, at least Dad died a peaceful death. He didn't have
to suffer on in one of those nursing homes. He wouldn't have wanted
that." Each of these statements is designed to alleviate our pain, just
a bit, and help us cope with the terrible loss that is now before us.

I do not mean to imply that rationalizations are always false or
untrue statements. On the contrary, there is much truth in the above
statements. Looking for the silver lining in tragic events can be a way
of empowering and uplifting our spirits. Rationalizations, like all defense mechanisms, are coping devices. Rationalizations distort reality, however slightly, and prevent us from seeing life as it now really
is. That may not be all bad, if we need a little fantasy to help us cope
for a while. But rationalizations can become walls behind which we
hide from our painful feelings. We know that healing lies in facing
the pain, in all of its fullness and implications. Healing lies in passing
through the pain, not in avoiding it. In time rationalizations should
give way to a fuller acceptance of truth and give birth to an affirma-
tion of life amid sorrow.

Idealization: Idealization is a process whereby a grieving person
idealizes that which is lost. Here too the griever may distort reality
to a degree. In idealization the griever momentarily forgets the negative attributes of the deceased or the favorite job or whatever he or

she has lost and focuses exclusively on the what is missed most about that which is lost. Almost all people in grief do some idealizing of what they have lost. Gradually, however, as the grieving process heals, one remembers a more realistic picture of that which is lost.

As a counselor who does considerable marriage counseling I am keenly aware of how many troubled marriages there are in this country. And even among the functional marriages, almost all couples have their points of tension, disagreement and regret. Yet, when I go to speak about grief at widows' meetings, I am fascinated by how many wonderful marriages there are in the world. The show of hands or the spontaneous sharing is amazing. Nearly every woman claims in some fashion that her dead husband was the most kind, loyal and devoted man she knew. Now I ask you, where did all of those troubled marriages go? Surely, the widows of troubled marriages may not be as likely to attend lectures on bereavement as are the widows who had positive marital relationships. It may also be that grief plays tricks on us all. The negative aspects of our marriages or marriage partners fade from view when the eyes are filled with tears.

Idealization, like other defense mechanisms, can be extreme or very modest in nature.[3] The more extreme idealization is, the more it distorts reality and the more disturbing and damaging it is to our mental health. Idealization, also like the other defense mechanisms, is normally more extreme in the early stages of grief and gradually gives way, as grieving continues, to the less extreme forms. And in time, if the grief process continues well, idealization is replaced by a realistic picture of the loss. The goal of grieving is to accept reality and to see life as it really was with all of the blemishes, all of the beauty and all of the ambiguities.

Reaction Formation: Reaction formation is a technical, psychoanalytic term for a type of defense mechanism whereby a person has an extreme opposite or displaced reaction to some unacceptable anxiety. I would like to broaden the term to include any attempt to run from pain by over-emphasizing the opposite. Sometimes when we feel the approaching pain of a loss, we run from it. We flee psychologically. Usually this "fleeing" is in an opposite sort of direction from that which we fear.

A woman in the mid-life years, for example, may fear that she is in danger of losing her job, that younger colleagues are passing her by. She responds by becoming more compulsive about her work, more of a workaholic, trying even harder to please the boss in every little way. Over-activity can be one way to avoid pain. Again, the key word is "over." Activity is not bad in itself, but only harmful if it prevents us from dealing with our feelings.

Consider the father who feels anxious about the impending loss of his adolescent children. With each passing year, they are getting older, more grown up, more independent. Soon they will be leaving home. He responds out of his own anxiety by clamping down even harder on his teenagers—more rules, more chores, higher expectations and tighter restrictions. Psychologically, he is trying to keep them at home, trying to keep them as children, trying to hold them close just a few more years. Unfortunately, this "controlling" can have the opposite effect. His children may rebel all the more, looking for every opportunity to express their independence or stay away from home. And the more they distance themselves from home, the more anxious dad becomes and the tighter the restrictions grow. This cyclic dynamic may escalate to the point of full-scale rebellion and require the intervention of a family therapist. Note that the problem began when the father avoided his own painful feelings by fleeing into the opposite. That's a type of reaction formation and it is a very common theme among those who grieve.

Regression: People can also flee or run away psychologically in countless other ways. Regression refers to a way of fleeing pain by going backward to a younger state of mind or way of acting. Drug and alcohol abuse has regressive themes to it, particularly when it is used to cope with loss experiences. Alcohol is a common way of deadening pain, calming fears and making reality go away. Alcohol is one way to anesthetize pain. It is no accident that most people's consumption of alcohol goes up during bereavement. The pain is gone temporarily. The next day, of course, the pain is there again. Pain never goes away permanently through any defense mechanism. Pain does not go away if you run away, but sometimes we need to anesthetize pain for a while ("we are buying some time"), while we build up our courage to face reality. If regression or any defense mechanism becomes permanent, then we have only encased pain, not eliminated it. We have ceased to grow, because we have failed to grieve.

This is one of the main ways that people become psychologically and spiritually crippled.

I hope that it is clear from this brief description of defense mechanisms that grief feelings are painful feelings and that one way to understand the different approaches people have to grief is to view their behavior as ways of coping with pain. This will be an important observation to keep in mind as we approach a discussion of loss and grief in later life. By the time we have reached the second half of life, most of us have some pretty well established ways of coping with emotional pain. Some of these ways may be pretty healthy; other coping mechanisms may not be so helpful. In general the pain needs to be dealt with emotionally if we wish to be healed. Each person, however, will find a different approach and pace to that process. Most successful grieving is a gentle combination of "facing the pain" and "distancing from the pain," a process that gradually moves toward restoration.

The Process of Grieving

What is probably clear by now is that grief is a process. This is a fairly simple, but important concept. Grief does not stay the same from day to day or week to week. It moves. It changes. It is like a journey down a winding road, wherein each turn in the path reveals a new landscape . . . or a landscape that you thought you left three stages ago.[4] The critical issue is to keep moving down the path. The temptation is always to retreat to a safe spot. Yet healing comes only as we continue down that pathway, "through the valley of the shadow of death," and we move through this valley only by regularly processing our feelings.

What makes this grieving journey even more interesting and complex is the mixture of other emotions that get added into the process. "Grief" itself, pure and simple, is probably the feeling of longing, sorrowing and hurting. But the "grief process" is a collection of feelings and emotions, of which grief is the most dominant, but not the only emotion. The following are some of the more common emotional companions.

Anger is a common element in grief, especially when the loss is unwanted. We protest. We argue. We get mad at everyone and everything. We look for someone upon whom to fix blame. We feel angry that our loved one was taken from us, or that we cannot work anymore, or that our children do not call us as often as they should or that our bodies do not work the way they used to. Anger is a normal feeling in bereavement, but a hard one for many people to acknowledge and allow themselves to express.

Depression is also a fellow traveler with us along the road of sorrow. Depression comes on us because we hold in some of that anger. We internalize it instead of expressing it. We may feel angry with ourselves or at the deceased or at God—all of whom are uncomfortable objects to be angry at. Periods of depression are common in bereavement, but they usually lift as the feelings are expressed and processed.

Despair is a close cousin to depression. Despair is more future oriented than depression. There are times in bereavement when we may come to feel hopeless about life. Our future now looks bleak, limited and dark. We have lost the one thing or one person we loved most. Despair particularly in old age is much harder to cure than depression. Ultimately there is no cure other than that cure that comes when we pass into a new stage of life and embrace life again as "good." Unfortunately, many people in later life, as I will suggest, do not make those many transitions and gradually sink into a chronic state of despair.

Guilt is another inevitable emotion in sorrow. Humans want to know why something tragic happened. "Why" questions reflect our desire to understand our personal responsibility in the events that have transpired. We ask, "What did I do wrong that caused this loss?" or "Did I say something I should not have?" or "Did I make the right decisions?" or the perpetual "What if" questions: "What if I had done this or said that?" "What if I had worked harder or driven safer or raised them differently—could this loss have been avoided?" These are all typical and inevitable questions. The situations vary, but the need to ask the questions remains. One of the on-going themes of "grief work" in later life is untangling the confusion people feel over their relative responsibility for past losses.

Anxiety and its more specific cousin, *fear*, are also present in grief. Anxiety comes to us first as a loss approaches. We anticipate losses. And as we do so, we get anxious. We do not wish to lose what we value. We do not want to be hurt. As I see my body change, I get anxious. As I watch my children grow up, I feel anxious. As I see younger work colleagues flourish, I feel anxious. All of these signs of approaching loss causes anxiety.

There is also a type of fear or anxiety that is present in bereavement that is after-the-fact. We worry about the unknown future that now lies before us because we have lost a loved one. We do not know what will happen to us now. "How will I cope now without her?" "How will I find enough money to live on in retirement?" "How will I get along with a crippled body?" "Will my children still love me after they leave?" These are the questions, prompted by fear, that linger in bereavement. The fear of loneliness, dependency, financial insecurity and declining health increase with every loss in the later years.

All of these feelings, along with grief itself, can be present in the "grief process." As with grief per se, the most critical factor in the resolution of these emotions is the full expression of these feelings. The more we talk out or express these feelings, the more our grief process will move along toward some resolution. The temptation is to hold it in, to be silently strong, to not want to bother anyone with our troubles, to run away from the painful sorrow or the angry reactions or the nagging guilt. Such temptations hamper our healing. As Jesus suggests in the second beatitude, only as we mourn will we find comfort (Mt 5:4). It is better to "go with the flow." Allow yourself to grieve, as fully and as completely as you can. Grief is much like a river that flows by itself toward the goal of restoration. Trying to block the river is difficult and ultimately self-destructive, but stepping into the river, flowing with our feelings, will move us along toward healing. In fact the more we go into grief, the easier and quicker we will come out of it. It is a strange but true paradox.

Grief and Meaning

Grief is a function of attachment. Humans have an innate "instinct" to emotionally attach ourselves to various people, objects, things, places. We care. That is part of the nature of being human.[5] Whenever we invest ourselves in something or someone, we infuse it with meaning. We say that we find it meaningful. We value it. We build our lives, our identities, our values around such "attachments." So, when we lose those attachments, for whatever reason, we must to some extent restructure our meanings, our values, even our identities. Grieving therefore can be understood as having a spiritual or theological dimension to it. That dimension can best be described as a process of giving up, readjusting and/or finding new meaning in one's life.

One of the most under-studied and little understood areas of life has to do with meaning. Humans, unlike other animals, have a "will to meaning."[6] We need to have a sense of meaning and purpose to our lives in order to be psychologically (and spiritually) healthy. Sometimes meanings are provided for us by our religion, our culture and/or other institutions. Some people find great meaning, for example, in their family. Others find meaning in their work. Others find it in their religious beliefs; still others, in an avocation or cherished cause. And still others find their greatest meaning to be in their appearance or financial status. Meaning is largely a subjective phenomenon. Individuals can get a sense of meaning and purpose in their lives from an infinite variety of sources, but the need for meaning is universal.

Parenthically, I am convinced more and more that one of the great spiritual illnesses of our modern times is meaninglessness. Most of the traditional sources of meaning—religion, nation, work and family—are changing rapidly and losing their ability to communicate values and command allegiance. Many of the traditional beliefs and symbols of meaning no longer relate to most people. In an increasingly pluralistic culture the problem is complicated even further. As a result, more and more modern, particularly urban, people are experiencing an existential emptiness. It is a frightening thing to realize that one's life is essentially meaningless, that one's life is really insignificant and that all of one's life work counts for naught. More and more people seem to feel this way, and seem to be on a search for a more lasting sense of purpose and meaning.

When we lose something that we have invested meaning in, we are temporarily thrown into what I call a "crisis of meaning." We are temporarily without this source of meaning. Our life may seem meaningless. Grief sufferers may say, "My life has no purpose, now that Susie is gone." Or "I feel so worthless now that I am not a contributing member of society." Or "It feels pointless to keep on living now that I can't care for myself. I'm only a burden on my family."

Most of us find our sense of meaning in life from several sources simultaneously. We have families, careers, hobbies, religious beliefs, political activities, etc. If we lose one of these areas, we have other areas of meaning to fall back on. But what about the man who has "put all of his eggs in one basket," for example, investing all of his worth into his career? Will it not be more difficult for him to adjust to retirement than for other men? Or what of the woman who has over-invested herself in her family and child-raising? Will it not be more difficult for her to adjust to the "empty nest" than for the woman who has also invested herself in a career or in some political/ social cause? Or consider the man who has over-invested himself in his appearance? To him looking healthy, trim and handsome is everything! How much more difficult it will be for him to deal with his loss of youth than for the man who also invested himself in a career, in his intellect and/or in family relations. My point is that losses create mini spiritual crises, and if what we have lost is central to our meaning system, then our crisis will be great. The meaning factor is an important element in understanding a person's grief reaction.

By the time most of us have reach age forty, we have some well-established meaning systems. Our meanings are usually focused around the major areas of life, like family, work, health, friends. Most of us know who we are, what we value and from where we derive our sense of purpose in life. But during the second half of life, we will suffer losses in each one of these major arenas of meaning: family, work, marriage, health, status, friends, etc. Inevitably then, these losses will lead us to revalue, rethink, redo our meaning systems. Each loss in later life carries with it this kind of spiritual or theological "crisis." We will ask questions such as "What is the meaning of this loss?" and "What does my life mean now that I am without what I've lost?" and "Can life be good again?" These questions reflect the spiritual "limbo" that most people feel themselves to be in while grieving. Finding answers to these questions is an important part of the healing process.

Grief in Later Life

Grief does seem to become more complex, more intense and more chronic in later life. There are some unique themes to loss and grief in the later years. As we enter those years ourselves or work with people going through those stages of life, we need to understand the uniqueness of grief in the later years. Here are some themes.

Rapidity of Losses: Losses come faster in later life. For example, consider the loss of a friend or relative by death. Although distant relatives die with some regularity, the death of a peer is a fairly rare event in early life. Yet after the passage of the mid-life point, we begin to notice that more of our peers die of heart attacks, accidents, cancer, even "natural causes." They are no longer rare, accidental events. And in old age, the death of peers becomes a regular occurrence. The longer we live, the more we experience the death of friends, peers and colleagues of the same age. Losses through death increase with the passage of time.

Consider also losses that we experience in terms of our health. Young people rarely experience a permanent loss of health. But as we grow older, we begin to notice minor physical limitations and annoyances. Still later, we experience the first semi-permanent or permanent loss of health. Perhaps we now need eye glasses. Perhaps our digestive tract needs regular assistance. Perhaps our bones now need muscle rub. Or the right ear needs a hearing aid. Each of these losses demands an adjustment from us. Barely have we adjusted to the last loss and a new one is upon us.

Losses seem to increase geometrically the longer we live. This makes the grieving process that much more complicated. Most people grieve slowly and incompletely, in spite of the best psychological advice to the contrary. That is O.K when there is only one loss a year, but what happens when there are three losses a year? Now the grieving process backs up! Barely we have adjusted to the last loss and the next one is upon us.

Roger was still adjusting to his mother's death when he was forced to take an early retirement for health reasons. Now he has three major losses he is dealing with, all within a short four year period. He used to say to me in the midst of all this, "One of these losses would have been enough for a guy like me to cope with. I really don't do very well with emotional stuff. Now I feel as though I have more than I can cope with." Roger was not coping well and the increased rapidity of losses in later life was catching up with him. He had to learn new, more rapid ways of coping with loss.

Losses come upon losses in later life—one grief, and then another. Some people, like Roger, just cannot keep up with it. It overwhelms their limited coping skills. Those that do learn to stay mentally healthy in later life do so because they learn or have learned to grieve rapidly and well.

Finality of Losses: Losses are more final in the later years. If we were to lose our spouse early in our life, there would still be time to remarry and resume a normal life. Yet, if we lose our spouse in the later years, there is less of a chance of remarriage. Women, for example, who lose their husband by divorce or by death after age fifty seldom remarry.[7] This is a fact that crosses the minds of many troubled couples who contemplate divorce after mid-life. Similarly, if a man loses his job or career in the early years of his life, it is a momentary hardship at worst. But if a man who is fifty-five years old or older loses his job, there is little time left to find a new career. Many men in this age bracket, who work for large competitive companies, are afraid to request even a small job change lest they give their employer the excuse "to let them go." "Who is going to want an individual with barely ten years of active employment left?" they reason. Their reasoning isn't all that unrealistic in today's competitive marketplace.

Losses in later life have this sense of finality to them that the losses of earlier life did not have. In fact, the sense of finality permeates all of the losses of later life, even the relatively minor ones.

The Ever-Present Character of Loss: Loss is more subtle and ever-present in later life. Loss of course is with us all the time, but in later life it seems as though there are fewer big dramatic losses and more of the gradual, subtle, constant losses. Most of the losses of later life are anticipated or should be. We know that someday our health will fail. Someday our spouse will pass on. Someday we will retire. There are often long periods of anticipation before these losses actually occur. This can be a very positive occurrence. It gives us time to prepare, if we will. But because the losses are more subtle, more diffuse, they are also easier to ignore for the person bent on avoidance. We can put off thinking about retirement or about what we are going to do when mother dies or where will we live when Sarah's eyes go. These are painful questions, easy questions to put off until tomorrow. We tend to put them off precisely because we don't want to deal with the feelings.

Losses surround us in later life. Losses are ever-present. Therefore grief is ever-present. Older people are almost in a constant state of grief. There is always a loss or two that they are adjusting to and always a loss or two just over the horizon that they are anticipating. Grief is a constant companion in the later years. The well-adjusted person in later life will learn to make friends with grief. In fact I would argue that if we want to age well through the second half of life we must become good grievers. We must learn to work through our ever-present grief.

Losses Are Cumulative: Losses become more cumulative in the later years of life. We have lived long enough now that losses build upon losses. It is not uncommon to attend a funeral in later life and find oneself crying, not over the current loss, but over an old one. The present grieving triggers past grieving in us. Current memories help us remember past hurts. Emotionally, losses seem to be linked together, like a long chain-linked fence.

This cumulative nature of loss and grief makes grieving more difficult in later life. We are not just grieving one loss, but several losses. With each passing year, many people leave more and more losses ungrieved. Most older adults walk about with many unresolved griefs. It is almost inevitable. Some losses can never be fully and completely resolved. What this does mean, however, is that most of us have grief feelings just below the surface of our psyches. Unconsciously, we know this and therefore seek to avoid funerals all the more. We fear that we could easily become overwhelmed by all of the hurt within us. This is the cumulative nature of losses in later life.

Loss Is Subjective

Loss is largely a subjective experience. Two people may experience the same event, but one person labels it a "loss" and the other person labels it a "transition." Every loss, even the most tragic, has some positive elements. Most losses actually carry with them a mixture of feelings—negative feelings of grief, sorrow, guilt and fear, and the positive feelings of relief, freedom, anticipation.

In addition, individuality increases with age. We are not all the same, and in fact we become more unique, the older we get. What this means is that the variety of ways people approach and experience loss also increases with age. Some people will look upon retirement as a loss; many others will see it as a blessing, and still others as simply a transition. The empty nest stage may be experienced by some adults as a negative thing and by others as a new-found sense of personal freedom. Some will mourn. Others will rejoice. Most will feel elements of both. What this also means is that no one's advice about losses in later life, especially mine, will apply uniformly to everyone. Everyone's experience is slightly different. I believe, however, that everyone's experience of loss in later life will involve some elements of grief. The grief may be more keenly felt at certain times than others. Inevitably it will be there, and unless or until it is dealt with, we cannot pass on into the next stage of life.

Perhaps "loss" is not the best word at all to describe the events of this book. Perhaps the word "transition" or "change" better characterizes the flavor of these events. Every loss is after all a change and a transition. Every loss carries with it "a demand," a requirement that we must change. But before we can change, we must first grieve the loss of what is now gone. Before we can go forward, we must go backward. Grieving comes first. Grieving makes growing possible.

Notes

1. The idea of varying degrees of denial was introduced to me in Avery D. Weisman, *On Dying and Denying: A Psychiatric Study of Terminality* (New York: Behavorial, 1972).

2. Another word for this type of denial might be repression.

3. In extreme forms, idealization becomes idolization. The two words have come to mean almost the same thing. I'll say more about this in the next chapter.

4. C.S. Lewis uses the image of grief as a journey in his description of his conjugal bereavement. See *A Grief Observed* (London: Faber and Faber, 1961).

5. This understanding of grief, as a function of attachment "instincts," is associated with the name John Bowley. See *The Making and Breaking of Affectional Bonds* (London: Tavistock Publications, 1979).

6. This is a phrase and philosophy that is associated with the name Viktor E. Frankl and his school of psychotherapy called "logotherapy." See *Man's Search for Meaning: An Introduction to Logotherapy* (Boston: Beacon Press, 1962).

7. This is due to a combination of factors: the preferred age differential between men and women, the shorter life span of men compared to women, as well as individual factors.

Chapter 2

Spiritual Health and Grief

"For where your treasure is, there will your heart be also" *(Mt 6:21).*

What does the model Christian look like? How would you describe the ideal religious person? In response to such questions, people of faith will paint widely differing pictures. There are probably as many different descriptions of this imaginary person as there are denominations or religious traditions. Each group, and maybe even each individual, will have an unique vision of the goal toward which we strive as pilgrims along the Way. The other interesting and related question is, "Does spiritual health change with the differing stages of life? Are the qualities that make one spiritually mature the same for the sixteen year old as they are for the forty-eight year old?" The question is certainly a complex one and also an intriguing one.

In this book I am going to propose a definition of spiritual health based on the concept of idolatry. Idolatry is a theme throughout the Scriptures and, in slightly differing forms, throughout the history of Christianity. It is a doctrine that gets at our basic understanding of God and human nature. It is a concept that both Jews and Christians can ascribe to as central to their understanding of God. Most importantly, it is a perspective on spiritual health that can transcend the differing stages of the life cycle. In this chapter I want to describe the basics of our theological understanding of idolatry, with an eye toward how this view of spiritual health might enrich our understanding of grief and loss in the later years.

Making Gods

Idolatry is simply the "worshiping of false gods." It is a theme that appears throughout the Old and New Testaments. It is there in the ten commandments, there in the fiery sermons of Ezekiel, there in the Maccabean revolt, there in Jesus' teachings against Pharisaic legalisms, and there in Paul's advice to Gentile Christians. All of Scripture could be understood as God's struggle with humans over idolatry. Humans seem to fashion idols for themselves over and over again. Each time the false gods get the upper hand, God breaks through our idolatry, calling us to a renewed faith in God alone. These brief periods of freedom, however, seem to be only interludes before we again fashion some new kind of idol.

In the period of the Old Testament literature people literally fashioned concrete idols out of clay or stone, which is where the term "idol" comes from. These statues were concrete visualizations of the imagined gods, be they the wind or rain or the gods of Canaan or the gods of fertility or prosperity. There were usually many gods, each having its own "turf" or area of authority. In a sense the battle between faith and idolatry, especially during Israel's years as a nation, was a battle between monotheism and polytheism. There were periods when both theological systems co-existed. People believed that "the Lord God is one," but they also visited local shrines and paid homage to lesser gods. Idolatry was also a nationalistic issue in ancient Israel. Monotheism was Israel's religion, whereas the religions of Israel's neighbors were polytheistic. The plea to return to a faith in one God often had nationalistic overtones. Abhorrence to idols and idolatry runs deep within the veins of Judaism and Jews.

In the Gospels we find few clay statues, but idolatry is just as critical an issue. Now idolatry takes the more subtle, but equally powerful forms of legalism, greed, lust and false allegiances. When Jesus confronts the rich young ruler (Lk 18:18–30), he is challenging him to give up his worship of wealth. When Jesus preaches to the scribes and Pharisees, he calls them to replace the god of legalism with a true faith in a God that transcends the law. People may not be publicly "bowing down" before idols, but they still are creating and worshiping false gods in their hearts. They may attend formal worship services for the one God, but their informal, daily allegiances are elsewhere. Again, we find idolatry and faith existing side by side and the struggle between the two continuing on into the Christian period. Now, the battleground is no longer the institutional structures of religion and state, but the hearts, lives and souls of individual persons. The issue is no longer the concrete idols, but the human tendency to create and worship false gods.

Biblical history can be characterized as a constant struggle between idolatry and faith, between worshiping the false gods and worshiping the "the living God." The form of the struggle changes slightly with each generation, but the struggle continues.

Let me raise the question then, "Why is there such a struggle at all? Why don't humans learn their lesson once for all?" Humans don't learn because there is something about human nature that drives us "to make gods." Repeatedly, over and over again, humans create false gods to worship. Even when we have formally pledged our allegiance to the living God, we still can't stop ourselves from this tendency to create and cling to false gods. I would suggest, as do the Scriptures, that humans need idols/false gods. "Idol making" is fueled by our innate insecurity with human existence itself, with our creatureliness, with our perceived powerlessness over the forces that control us. Fueled by this anxiety, we are driven "to idolize."

Anything, even good things, can be made into a god, especially in the context of bereavement. I was asked once by the conference minister to intercede as a meditator in a dispute between two segments of a local church. These kind of "church wars" are always difficult to deal with. The two segments of the congregation were divided sharply around the issue of pastoral leadership. One group in the congregation was extremely loyal to the former minister who had been at that congregation for eighteen years, and who had retired the previous year and then unexpectedly died two months later. The other group was supportive of the new cleric, who was struggling to find his own identity amid a congregation that was dominated by the ghost of Rev. "Billy" Larson. There were other issues operating here as well. The former group was largely older in years; the latter group, younger in years. The former group was made up of the longer-term members; the latter group were mostly newer members. And there were some individual grudges that were getting thrown into the mix too. All in all it was quite a war, a war that threatened to split the congregation right down the middle.

The particular trigger for this conflict was a request by the group loyal to the former pastor to rename the church after that pastor. The church would be called, "Larson Memorial Christian Church." It was a wonderful suggestion, a noble tribute to a man who had given so much of his life serving these people. The current pastor, supported by the other segment of the congregation, discouraged the idea. To him it seemed a bit too much, "rather as though we are glorifying the dead or something." His remarks were met with anger and hurt by the former group, who could easily recount story upon story of the wonders of Pastor Billy. The current pastor was reluctant to "put his foot down." He didn't want to lose this older, more influential segment of the congregation—but neither did he want the church renamed after his predecessor.

These kind of situations are not easily resolved, and this one was particularly difficult. A compromise was found eventually that saved the church's unity, but not without the price of a few members. However I remember being impressed with how easily even believers can idolize ("make little gods of") even good people. In this case the process was fueled by the pain of grief and idealization of the deceased. Release and wholeness came only when God broke through to several mourning members, with a vision of faith in Christ that transcends loyalty to persons.

Religious people are not immune from this tendency to create and worship false gods. Even though we formally worship the living God, we can nevertheless create one or many "little gods" that in fact may have more influence in our lives than the true God. The Christian walk is a constant struggle to stay on the "straight and narrow path" and avoid the many temptations to worship elsewhere.

Temporary Gods

Idolatry occurs when something that is less than God is set up as a god. Nearly anything can be made into an god. In ancient times it was the attributes of nature—there were sun gods and gods of thunder and gods that dwelt in the ocean depths. Political entities could also be made into gods. Caesar was treated like a god, as were the pharaohs of Egypt. Desired qualities can become gods. There were fertility gods that bestowed children and/or a good harvest on their devoted subjects. Beauty might be made into a little god and would hopefully grant beauty to its faithful. In more modern times, we find people who worship success, fame, power, status and wealth. They live for their gods just as surely as the ancients did for theirs.

Whether ancient or modern, however, idols are always things that are essentially temporary, not eternal. Rulers die. Fame fades. Success is short-lived. And fertility is only for a season. Idols are false gods precisely because they are finite. They are of this world. Yet by making these things into gods, we hope they will become infinite. We hope that they will last forever. Of course, they never do. They are relative, not absolute; temporary, not permanent.

Marlene sat in my office sobbing. She was a broken woman, a desperate woman. She cried out, "Nobody! Nobody will take me seriously, doctor. I am more than a cute face and a big set of boobs. I have a brain! I have an intellect. I have a soul." Yes, that is what Marlene was missing, a soul. As she poured out her history, she told me that from day one in her life, she was told how cute she was. She was the apple of her parents' eye, the youngest and prettiest of six children. She was fussed over. She was fixed up. She was admired. She was entered in all of the beauty contests and usually won. Always she was expected just to stand there and look pretty. Don't say anything. Don't do anything. Just look good. And so she did. As she grew into adulthood, she incorporated those values. She too worshiped at the altar of appearance. She spent hours in front of the mirror, among the clothes' racks and in the beauty salons.

The only trouble with this scheme was that Marlene grew older, and at thirty-eight her beauty was "dull" compared to the sparkling looks of younger women. She began to have a growing sense of emptiness, at times even of panic. Part of her wanted it back—the attention, the youth, the admiration. Part of her was angry—angry that it deluded her, angry that she couldn't stay young no matter how hard she tried, angry that she had nothing else going for her. The cruelty was that she both hated it and loved it. Her beauty was her blessing and her curse.

It was hard for Marlene to break free from the grip of this false god, particularly in a society that worships at the same altar. Her liberation however began when she started to see that the god was temporary, not permanent. Freedom emerged when she began to see that the god's power was waning. Then, and only then, did she begin to reclaim her power.

The fact that false gods are essentially temporary in nature, in contrast to the living God who is eternal, is a helpful distinction to keep in mind as we approach a discussion of loss in later life. Most of what we grieve over in life are "attachments" which are temporary in nature. We know that someday our health will decline, our job will be terminated, our children will grow up and our parents will pass on before us. We know these things. That doesn't stop us, nor should it stop us, from continuing to love such things. But when these attachments are taken from us, it should help us resist the temptation to make them into "little gods."

Gods You Can Touch

Another central feature of idolatry is that these lesser gods are almost always concrete or visible entities. They are things of this world, things that can be directly touched, seen or grasped. The stone carved idol can be touched. The fury of the ocean can be seen. The armies of imperial Rome can be grasped. False gods are false precisely because they are visible, concrete things of this world. You may recall Isaiah's satire against idolatry in which he describes how the idol maker fashions the idol out of wood and metal and then "falls down to it and worships it and prays to it, 'Deliver me, for thou art my god' " (Is 44). Isaiah correctly notes that idols are always concrete entities. That is their falsity, but it is also their lure. Their concreteness makes it possible for humans to relate to these gods. They can be captured, held, possessed, even owned.

Idols, the visible representation of false gods, are concrete, but, more than this, the rewards of worshiping false gods are also concrete. If we worship the god of power, we hope to gain the tangible benefits of status, money and control over our future. If we worship the god of a particular social cause, we hope to see results of that movement's progress in the real world. And if we worship the subtle god, called "being a good boy" (or girl), we expect to reap the rewards of staying out of trouble and avoiding conflict. It is little wonder then that idols have their appeal. Their rewards are much more real, tangible and useful than those of an invisible God.

The concrete nature of false gods stands in contrast to the living

God, who is essentially invisible. "God is fundamentally, essentially invisible," writes Jacques Ellul.[1] "Over and over again it is proclaimed and stated that no one can see God and live." Even Moses sees God only from behind, as God passes by. No one can see God's face. Normally, we "see only God's trace after he has passed by: God's work and God's action after the fact."[2] Worshiping this kind of God requires great trust. It is much easier for humans to worship the false gods, who are more concrete and whose benefits are more tangible.

Among all of the most popular false gods today, none is more real, down-to-earth, than money. Bill was particularly prone to the idolization of money. He was raised in a poor home and "had to do without" over and over again. He came to resent being poor and vowed that he would never be such again. After a brief period at college, he left college for the real world of stock trading. He enjoyed the challenge of achievement and the chance to make a fortune. He began by cleaning rooms at night. He studied hard. He asked questions. He learned the business and advanced regularly. When I met Bill he was approaching mid-life and "just about had it made." He had a personal portfolio that was going to enable him to retire comfortably at age fifty, if he just made one or two more big trades.

The temptation was just too great. He began to do what every stock trader does at some time or another. He began to cut corners—register stocks at different prices than they were actually sold for. A common practice? "Everyone does it," he thought. He got caught and was fired from his job after twenty-three years in the business. He was shattered. He was depressed—but he couldn't let go. He couldn't just walk away—the fear of being poor was too great. It drove him to run the risk again, take that last chance. When I last heard from Bill, he had got another job in the same line of work and was moving up the ladder again, still gripped by the vision of "never being poor again." He couldn't see that there was anything else to life, anything else that was so concrete. I wondered when the next crisis would be.

Jacques Ellul's book *Humiliation of the Word* has offered us a provocative discussion of idolatry in the context of modern technological society. Ellul has argued that God is essentially a God of the word and that idolatry always involves a substituting of something visible for something heard. Modern technological societies are increasingly "humiliating" the spoken word in favor of the visible image, says Ellul. Humans seem to find the visible image easier to relate to, to grasp and to manipulate. The God of Israel, however, is essentially invisible and therefore unable to be manipulated. Worshiping this God requires more trust, even more faith, than worshiping the visible gods of this world. False gods are always ones that we can see and touch and from which we derive some tangible benefit. This very quality makes them false.

False Promises

All gods promise salvation. That is part of the definition of godhood. Gods are sources of salvation. God or gods save us from something dreadful, something we cannot save ourselves from. False gods or idols also promise salvation. That's their lure. That's the bait. The false god always says in so many words, "If you worship me, I will give you all this . . . " The "goodies" may include protection, as from accidents or illnesses or nature's fury. The goodies may be rewards, as a greater harvest or prosperity or a long life. The goodies also may be transcendence or fame or power or "the good life."

The false god's appeal is always to something we need or feel we need to survive. Most of these needs, in proper perspective, are normal human needs. We need food, safety, self-esteem, love and a sense of transcendence. The idol's lure is that one or more of these needs will be ultimately satisfied once and for all. We need no longer live "by daily bread." Now, we can have it all and have it forever. Finally, we will be genuinely happy. Salvation is just around the corner, if . . .

Television commercials are an interesting commentary on our society. They reflect and sometimes create the needs and the idols of our culture. It is enlightening to examine the promises that television commercials make and the hidden god that they invite us to worship. Consider these samplings:

• The beer commercial that shows happy people, having fun, partying together. What does it promise? It promises friendship, if we drink their beer. Is that where friendship is found? What is the god? The god is consumption, alcohol or pleasure.

- The new car commercial shows a person (happy, of course) speeding around curves and over highways and byways. What is the lure? Power, a sense of mastery over the environment, and in a sense over ourselves. What is the hidden god? Control? Worship the god of control and be in command of your life!

- The Christmas toy commercials show children opening gifts, responding to the generous parent with kisses and praise. What is the promise? That your children will love you if you buy them these toys. Can love be purchased? Some god would want to us to believe so.

- The shaving cream commercial that shows a man shaving his beard without pain and a sexy woman admiring his smooth skin. What does this product promise? Not just a clean shave, but sex appeal. If you smell right, look right, feel right, you will be desirable. What is the god that they invite you to worship? Sexual satisfaction? Popularity?

Most of us who have been born since 1950 have been raised on television commercials. Researchers say that by the time we are eighteen years old, we have watched 17,000 hours of commercials.[3] That is a lot of brainwashing. These false gods have wonderful marketing programs. The promises seem so inviting. If only they were true.

It would be naive for us to say that false gods do not exist. They do exist and yet they don't exist. This is what Ellul calls the "paradox of idols." They exist in the sense that they exercise power over individuals. They control. They influence. They enslave. They do all of this precisely because they offer salvation. And yet . . . they don't exist. They are human creations. They are temporary, limited, finite and concrete. Their promises are therefore short-sighted, limited and only for the day.

A Cadre of Slaves

All of us have our little obsessions. Surely. It is a manner of degree. Most reasonable people can resist the temptation to get too caught up in the worship of false gods. Others cannot. Did you ever look closely at people caught in the trap of idolatry? There is a compulsivity in such people. They are intense, serious, driven to make their sacrifice. There is little humor or frivolity in their lives, especially about their "ultimate concern."

There is a sense that these people are psychologically slaves. Instead of freeing humans, these gods seem to entrap us. They make us slaves. Clinically this happens because false gods essentially fail to produce the promised salvation, but they do give us just enough to keep us "hooked."[4] If you are an ancient person, who is worshiping the river god and faithfully tossing your sacrifice upon the river once a month, the river responds positively often enough (pure probability) that you are encouraged to do it again. If the river does not respond or floods your farm, then you conclude: "I must have done something wrong. I'll try a bigger sacrifice next month." If you are a modern person who is worshiping the god of perfectionism, you can be perfect just often enough to be pleasing—but never perfect enough. And if you cannot be perfect, well then, "It must be because I didn't try hard enough, or didn't organize my time well enough, or . . . whatever." Next time I'll be perfect.

People who are worshiping false gods have this driven quality about them. They are desperate, addicted, narrowly focused. The false god becomes their whole life. It consumes all of their energies. All other values and priorities fade in comparison.

Karen was one such person. She was a perfectionist. She was a nurse by trade and a good nurse at that. She was head nurse of a demanding section of a major metropolitan hospital. Her perfectionism worked well at the hospital, where everything could be neatly organized, the rounds could be efficiently scheduled and each job thoroughly completed. The doctors and hospital administrators, who were minor perfectionists themselves, heaped praise upon Karen for her work.

Fortunately (or unfortunately) Karen's religion fed into this driving perfection. She was a lifelong, active member of a conservative, moralistic church that had extensive instructions on how to live a Christian life. It taught her proper beliefs, healthy foods, financial planning, sexual morals, family devotionals and so on. There weren't too many areas of Karen's life that weren't controlled or guided by her church. All that suited her fine. She enjoyed the sense of satisfaction in seeing a job done well and righteously. Her life was well ordered, disciplined and above reproach.

The only area of Karen's life that wasn't working for her was her home life. Karen's perfectionism drove her husband crazy. He was by nature a much more casual, relational and even disorganized person. In the early years of their marriage, it really didn't bother him if she wanted to be superwoman. As the children grew in years and discipline became an issue, however, their two parenting styles clashed head-on. Karen wanted the children's lives well organized, managed for success and on time. Bob's concern was more that the children enjoy themselves, "After all," he would say, "they are only kids once."

It seemed like with the passing of each year, Karen's need for perfection at home only increased. She became more and more demanding, nagging and pushing. In return, Bob became more of a passive aggressive, saying "Sure, sure honey . . . " but then doing nothing. This only aggravated Karen and made her push harder, to which Bob responded by slowing down even more. The children were caught in the middle and soon learned to play one parent against the other.

Merle R. Jordan has suggested in his new book that pastoral counseling can be defined as a process of "taking on the gods."[5] People who are disturbed are such because they have given allegiance to some false god that falsely defines who they are and distorts their values and relationships. All of us, says Jordan, have an operational theology that may stand in contrast to our formal or professed theology. Our operational theology includes the beliefs that we actually operate our lives by. Karen operated her life by the belief that "I am not a worthwhile person unless I am good enough." Unfortunately she could never be completely good enough. So the terror of being worthless drove her . . . and drove her. She never got better until she stopped, turned around, looked the terror in the face and challenged her basic operational belief about her worthlessness. In short, she never got better until she was willing to "take on the gods."

God Seeks After Us

The true living God hates idolatry. God is exclusive, even jealous. This is the message that Scripture gives us over and over again. Idolatry angers God. God created humans to be free, not slaves. God created humans for living relationships, not sterile robot relationships with cold pieces of stone. God also is angry that some of his children prefer slavery to freedom. God made us for better.[6] God also made us free, free to choose slavery over freedom . . . yes free even to be slaves. According to the Bible, God has not given up on us. God works actively to lure humans away from the worship of false gods. Sometimes that luring is gentle and gradual. Sometimes it is dramatic and traumatic.

Johnny drank most all of his life. His brother drank and his father drank. And Johnny could recount story after story of what fun he had drinking at college parties. In those days it never occurred to him that this was a problem. Initially his wife drank as well. That's what he liked about her. However, after the children came, she "got religion" and sobered up, but all of her efforts failed to get him to sober up too. After all Johnny "never took orders from any female," and he "could stop any time he really wanted to."

Johnny's addiction was a special kind of slavery. It was more than a psychological and spiritual addiction, although it was that too. After years of drinking, Johnny was also addicted physically to booze. The "demon" had a special grip on him, on his body as well as on his psyche and his soul.

There were many people who tried gentle ways of luring Johnny away from the booze. His pastor spoke to him. His doctor warned him. His wife nagged him. He business partners advised him. None of these ways worked. The only one who got to him was his seven year old daughter, lying in the hospital room, when she said, "Daddy, will you stop drinking? You are hurting me." That did it! That and the fact that he had almost killed her in a car accident because he wasn't clear-headed enough to react to the other car that was running a red light. The driver of that car, ironically, was booked for drunk driving. Now, Johnny has stopped drinking. With the help of the A.A. program, he knows that he can never drink again. And if that wasn't enough, he has only to look at the scar on his daughter's arm to remind himself again.

God doesn't intend that anyone, especially a seven year old child, be injured or crippled. Then again, idolatry carries with it its own judgment. Sometimes that judgment is harsh. For Johnny, looking at it now from the vantage point of years of sobriety, it was a measure of grace, not judgment. Now Johnny believes that nothing else would have worked, would have broken him of his fierce addiction to alcohol. "God never gave up on me," tells Johnny. "He kept after me. And when gentle ways did not work, God had to be rough with me . . . nothing else would have done it." God is persistent about those he loves.

Idolatry and Abnormal Grief

As has been noted in Chapter One, every loss, no matter how major or minor, forces us to enter into a grieving process. We mourn for what we have lost. Most people recover well enough. Others do not. Perhaps you have met a few people who remain in grief beyond a reasonable period of time. Such people still cling to the past, longing for the return of the deceased spouse, the lost career, the youthful appearance, the physical potency, in short, "the good old days." These people get locked in by their sorrow, trapped, even enslaved.[7] These people believe that the only happiness they have ever known or will know was back then, in what is now lost. The future looks bleak. They would rather live in the past.

Clinically, abnormal grief has all of the characteristics of idolatry. If we cannot successfully grieve the loss of something or someone, we may make it into an idol. We may idealize it beyond all semblances to what it really was. We "idolize" it. We long for it. We want it back. We believe that it alone will give us happiness, only if it returns . . . or only if we continue to give it our allegiance. We can't let go. The more intense our fixation becomes, the more driven by it we are. We may become consumed by the loss. Nothing else matters. Our priorities, our values are altered to accommodate this obsession with the past. It has become our god, our false god.

What people who are stuck in abnormal grief fail to see of course is that they have "idolized" their loss. The lost person or entity, no matter how dear it is to them, has become a false god. It is false because first it is not infinite. Oh, how they wished it were so, but it is temporary, as all of life on earth is temporary. It died. Or it left. Or they grew away from it. No matter. The important thing is that it is gone. It is gone—but it is not gone. It still controls their lives. It still consumes their energies. It promises them a type of salvation that reads, "If only I could recapture what I lost, then I would be happy." Unfortunately, in the process of idolizing, the persons stuck in grief have "deadened" something else—themselves. They too have stopped living.

Not everyone gets this obsessed by grief or has an abnormal mourning experience. Yet to some extent the choice between idolatry and faith is there for all of us each time and every time we face a new loss. To some extent each of us, in every major loss, experiences elements of abnormal grieving. Each loss calls us to give up something, something that we valued, loved and needed so dearly. Each loss forces us to emotionally let go of that which we loved. Each loss forces us to let go of the past, the temporary past and move into the future. We may not do so willingly or joyfully, but move into the future we must. For healing and spiritual wholeness lie only in the future, the ever-present future that unfolds before us.

Spiritual Health in Later Life

As I indicated earlier it is very hard to formulate a definition of spiritual health that will transcend the various stages of the life cycle. Obviously, what may be spiritually appropriate for an individual at age twenty may be different than what spiritual maturity would look like at age sixty-five. Nevertheless, idolatry offers us a perspective on spiritual health that is relevant to every stage of life. At every age people have to choose between faith in the living God and faith in false gods. In bereavement the temptation "to idolize" is acute. To a greater or lesser extent all of us are lured by this natural temptation, augmented as it is by the equally natural defense mechanisms of bereavement.

The spiritually mature person has faith.[8] This faith allows one to grieve, to let go, to release what is lost. Being able to grieve easily and relatively quickly is a very important quality in later life. As we will see, the losses come more rapidly and with more severity in the second half of life. If we wish to remain psychologically healthy through this difficult period of life, we must be able to grieve well. Faith is an essential ingredient in our ability to grieve. We cannot grieve well without it.

Each time we experience a new loss, we are faced with a choice between faith in a living God that pulls us into the future and faith in false gods that keep us enslaved to the past. In every loss, whether it be of our spouse, our health, our job or our youth, we are tempted "to make idols" out of what was lost. We are tempted in one form or another not to grieve. But by grieving we let go of that past, of that which is now lost, and free ourselves to move into the future. There in the future, God waits for us, longing to make life good again.

Notes

1. Jacques Ellul, *The Humliation of the Word* (Grand Rapids: William B. Eerdmans, 1985), p. 93.

2. This is why the Christian message is so unique. In Christ, Christians claim to see God for the first time. God has taken human form precisely so he can be visible to us.

3. See R.M. Lieberf, J.M. Neale and E.S. Davidson, *The Early Window: Effects of Television on Children and Youth* (New York: Pergamon, 1973).

4. Behavorial psychology tells us that sometimes the occasional reinforcer is more effective than a constant reinforcer.

5. See Merle R. Jordan, *Taking on the Gods: The Task of the Pastoral Counselor* (Nashville: Abingdon, 1986).

6. For the most part I have tried to avoid sexist language. The use of masculine pronouns in referring to God clearly does not imply a masculine nature of God, but simply conforms to universal custom.

7. Abnormal grief does not have to be characterized by just sorrow. Undue bitterness, depression or guilt can also be a sign of an unfinished grief process.

8. The last chapter of this book will offer a more extensive discussion of the role of faith in grief and successful aging in the later years of life.

Chapter 3

The Loss of Youth

"So teach us to number our days that we may get a heart of wisdom" (Ps 90:12).

Like all of the losses described in this book, the loss of youth begins in a gradual way and then escalates with each passing year. It is hard to know exactly when and where particular people no longer feel young, when it is that they begin to think of themselves as old or middle-aged or elderly. It is mostly a subjective change, one that can occur at nearly any age, but does occur regularly in later life. Usually the first awareness of this loss occurs during the mid-life years, as the individual passes from the first half of life to the second. From then on the loss of youth is a perceptual theme of life.

The Changes of the Body

Usually the first awareness of the loss of youth comes with changes in one's body. These are subtle changes. At first they are ignored. They are passed off as momentary limitations. All I need to do is "get back in shape" or "get over this bug that's going around" or "go on a strict diet." But the changes become persistent and in time the signs get clearer, more unmistakable. Their message becomes harder and harder to avoid.

Can you remember when and where you first realized that you were no longer young? When did you first realize that you were getting older? Perhaps you used to be able to eat pizza and drink beer late at night and sleep like a baby. Then pizza at night started keeping you awake. The digestive tract changed. Did you have a similar experience with coffee? No longer can you have that late night cup of coffee unless you want to be up half the night.

Where else did you first notice it? Perhaps one day you didn't bound up the stairs like you used to? You were winded. It was either that those stairs got longer or you have gotten old. Probably the latter. Your body has changed. Remember when your muscles first got sore after a little game of softball in the neighborhood? Or how your legs ached when you tried a pirouette? The body has changed again. Remember when it became harder to study large quantities of material? You just couldn't memorize the way you used to. The mind had changed—that was the scary one.

I remember the day that my twelve year old daughter challenged me to a race back to the beach blanket. That used to be an easy thing. In fact I usually had to slow myself a bit in order to make it more exciting. After all, the fun was in the thrill of beating dad. I remember the day that I stopped pacing myself. She kept getting faster and faster. I kept speeding up, faster and faster, or at least so I thought. I couldn't keep up. I was trying as hard as I could, but the old legs were not moving as fast as they might. When we both flopped down on the beach blanket, I slightly after she, my diplomatic wife causally remarked, "Well, I guess you are not as young as you used to be." It was a casual remark, a nothing remark, but for me it was one of those moments when suddenly you saw it all. "One day will make you old."[1]

Not only do the inner workings of the body change, but the outward appearance of the body does as well. The hair begins to show signs of graying or balding or both. The waistline begins to grow steadily outward. The hips widen. The smile lines become permanent. The cheeks droop. The curves aren't where they used to be. The firmness gives way to softness. Of course, we can do more to remake the outward appearance of the body. Trendy clothes, a nice hair style, even a face lift—all do wonders to make one feel youthful and "in step" with the times. It is easy to pretend the body isn't changing.

The decline or change in our appearance is an insidious thing. It strikes so keenly at our vanity. We do need to feel sexually attractive and socially appealing, and to be less so is a change that is hard to take. When did you notice that people started treating you differently? You flirt with the young girl in the supermarket, and she not only doesn't flirt back, but she has that look on her face as though she is humoring you. Oh, how painful! It's walking down the street, thinking you look like a million bucks and secretly wanting to be noticed—and nobody does! How the arrows of fading beauty sting.

All this comes on us gradually at first. Then over the years of later life, bodily changes become a regular theme. Every year some new change emerges. Every year or so our body tells us again that it has changed and we had better change too. With each passing year the physical changes become more pronounced and more negative. When we do have an illness or surgery, it now takes longer and longer for our bodies to recover. We use to bounce back within a few days. Now it's a few weeks. The bottom line is that we must make adjustments—adjustments in our lifestyle, in our diet, in our expectations of ourselves physically. In order to make these adjustments, we must first face the reality of our loss of youth and grieve its passing. Only then, after we have worked through the cognitive and emotional elements, are we motivated to make the necessary behavioral adjustments.

Marker Events

The first awareness of the loss of youth comes on us gradually. It sneaks up on us emotionally. At a certain level we know changes are occurring, but we block their full conscious impact. We make minor adjustments and go on pretending. The full awareness of the loss comes to us in what are called "marker events."[2] A marker event is a social event that symbolically marks the passing of time, the transition from one life stage to another. There are lots of marker events. Almost any event can be an "eye opening experience" if the timing is right. One's fortieth birthday is usually such an event. Our child's graduation or first date or new driver's license can also be a marker event. Or maybe a divorce or a career change crystallizes these changes and makes us fully aware of our loss of youth.

High school class reunions are weird events. Reunions take many shapes and forms. Usually they are dinner dances. There is a photographer there to take an updated picture of the class of '63 or whatever. There are lots of decorations and tales from the "good old days" which have gotten better with each telling of the story. Nostalgia drips off the walls. But the most important thing is the people, the faces and the names. Most of us come frightened and fascinated to see just how our classmates have changed. Some people are the same—just the same. It is amazing—just larger versions of the same face. Others are better. That timid, shy girl with the horned rimmed glasses—wow! She's now stunningly attractive and socially poised. She's holding court over by the bandstand. Nobody can believe it. And some are worse. Remember the boy who was such a "fox" in high school? Now he's just another middle-aged man with a beer gut, a balding head and a foul mouth. In some ways he hasn't grown up at all. And with sighs of relief you can hear his former admirers saying, "I'm glad I didn't marry him." Yes, class reunions are weird events, or better said, events that evoke weird feelings.

I can appreciate why people tend to avoid class reunions. The event planners say that you're lucky if half of the former class shows up. Many people are just too busy. Many have gone on to other relationships and other places. Most just want to avoid the whole thing. Reunions force us to deal with our past, who we were and by implication who we are now. Reunions can be one of those marker events that help us crystallize how far we have come—or haven't. They make us look at ourselves and face the reality that we are no longer young. Most of us come away from class reunions with feelings—relief, fear, fascination and of course, grief. Reunions force us to grieve for the loss of our youth.

We have relatively few socially prescribed marker events in modern urban life.[3] The rituals of former days have faded in the face of the rising tide of secularism and pluralism. The absence of marker events makes it all the easier to avoid dealing with our loss and sorrow. Yet the feelings do sneak up on us. Grief feelings have a way of looking for places to come to the surface. Sometimes when we least expect it or in the seemingly happy events, we are overcome by a sense of sorrow. Then for a moment, perhaps just a moment, we are fully aware of what we have lost.

The Changing Career

Individuals who have worked in a career all of their lives tend to measure the passing of their lives in terms of their work. "Young" and "old" get defined by the career, not by the person. When did you cease to be "a rising star" in your chosen career and start being treated like "a seasoned veteran"? When did they begin to value you for your stability rather than for your vigor, for your loyalty to the company instead of for your creativity, for your stature instead of for your "fresh ideas"? The clues are subtle and differ in each professional group. Professional athletes are old at age thirty. Some people, like police officers or career military people, can retire after a brief twenty years of service. Executives with aerospace firms are "old" by fifty, because that is the age whereby it is cheaper for the company to hire a younger person just out of college rather than continuing to pay an executive level salary. Individuals in a trade or skilled labor notice their transition when they can't keep up with the physical demands of their job, when they start to instruct younger people instead of doing it themselves. Doctors, airline pilots, judges and diplomats seem to reach their peak only after age fifty. These are careers that value wisdom and maturity.

Peter was one of those brilliant young engineers fresh out of M.I.T. when he was sought after by several major construction firms. His doctoral work was in new structural designs for nuclear power plants, a timely and needed subject. His early years with Nash International Construction Co. included lots of travel and periods of international residency, supervising the construction of overseas projects. His work was appreciated by the company executives. He even wrote a modest article for a trade journal on his theories of design. As a result, Peter rose rapidly within the ranks of the company and his salary rose correspondingly.

After eighteen years of work at the ripe age of forty-eight Peter was transferred back to the home office, where his work focused more on supervision than on implementation. The company had grown some since those early days, and now it needed him back at home supervising the growing number of younger engineers and drafters. At first this was nice, being settled with his family, but after a while he grew bored and restless.

The awareness began slowly for Peter. Their were little signs, like the younger men referring to him as the "old man" or the way they referred to his once pioneering design theory, as "dated" or the way the CEO fussed over Dave Jackson, the newest man in structural work. Peter just felt useless, as though he was "a has been," as though he had been "put out to pasture." His career was plateauing. There hadn't been a merit increase in years and certainly not an advancement since . . . well, since he was placed in the home office. Yet, he had to admit to himself that part of him liked this more settled routine. It was easier on his family and on his nerves and part of him liked "fathering" the younger men and now women engineers. Yet, part of him also longed for the excitement, the challenge of being "on site," seeing the project completed. In his more depressed days he felt as though he was just waiting until retirement. He longed to do something new, something on the cutting edge. That's what led him to make inquiries.

He had to do something. He thought that a new job, perhaps with a new firm, would bring him more satisfaction, more of a challenge. Perhaps a new firm would appreciate him more. Yes, that is it, "appreciate." That's what he wanted, "to be appreciated." So he put out a few feelers. He was hopeful, upbeat. How could any company not be thrilled to get someone with his experience? He'd have no trouble getting a job, he fantasized, probably a better one than he currently had, and, yes, probably one with more of an opportunity for advancement. Maybe he could still be a vice president someday.

That was when he heard the word, really *heard* the word— the word "old." It was in the interview with the other firm's officers. Peter was confident, poised, but they were lukewarm. Uninterested. He couldn't believe it. A man with his credentials. Then they said it: "Pete you're a great guy. You've done some great things for this industry—but you're not on the cutting edge right now. We need younger fellows with newer ideas. The business has really gotten competitive, you know. Really competitive. It's really not worth it for us to meet your asking salary for someone as 'old' as you are."

It was funny, but it helped. It helped to hear the word "old." It hurt, but he felt better in a strange way. In a sense, now he knew. There was no more pretending. Now he felt freer too, freer to go back to Nash's and do what he was good at. It was as though he had "let go" of something, and in letting go he was free to be who he really was at this stage of his career.[4]

Loss of Dreams

When we are young we have plenty of dreams. We dream of being rich. We dream of being president of the company, bishop of the diocese, professor at the university, senator in the congress or owner and proprietor of The Village Hardware. We dream of having a white house in the suburbs, with a picket fence, three children and a vacation home in the mountains. We dream of publishing that novel, making that discovery or patenting that invention. We dream of that special someone who would make us happy. We dream of happiness, achievement and long years ahead. Some of our dreams were pretty unrealistic. Some of them were even illusional. Some were not. In any case our youth is filled with dreams.

The loss of youth is associated with the loss of dreams and vice versa. One of the signs of getting older, of passing beyond youth, is a painful realization that some of our dreams won't come true. Perhaps we have dreamed too much, fantasized beyond the point of realism. Maybe we have fulfilled some of our dreams—and perhaps the fulfilled dreams did not turn out the way they were supposed to. We spent years making a dream come true, only to be disappointed. Or perhaps we are still working for the fulfillment of some dreams. In any event it is becoming increasingly clear, as we get older, that some of our dreams may not be realized. Time is short now. We must let go of the dreams of youth. We must revise our "battle plan."

Judith Viorst, in her book, *Necessary Losses,* describes the many losses of the life cycle that are "necessary," losses that we must lose in order to grow into the next phase of life. Among these losses, she describes the loss of dreams and illusions during the late middle age period this way:

> And we may start to feel that this is a time of always letting go, of one thing after another after another: our waistlines. Our vigor. Our sense of adventure. Our 20/20 vision. Our trust in justice. Our earnestness. Our playfulness. Our dream of being a tennis star, or a TV star, or a senator, or the woman for whom Paul Newman finally leaves Joanne. We give up hoping to read all the books we once had vowed to read, and to go to all the places we'd once vowed to visit.

We give up hoping we'll save the world from cancer or from war. We even give up hoping that we will succeed in becoming underweight—or immortal.[5]

Fantasies, dreams and illusions are subtle things to lose. It is not like losing a home or a spouse or a damaged leg. These are not concrete entities. Nevertheless, they are very real, very powerful and very determinative to our well-being. See, most of us fashion our identities around our dreams. We build a sense of who we are based on our dreams. We plan our life's script around the dreams that we feel we are supposed to fulfill. And our self-esteem rises or falls with the achievement of these dreams. We cannot "live" without dreams. Humans are dreamers. This is why the loss of dreams that comes with later life can invoke such subtle but powerful feelings.

Eschatology and Loss

As people pass over the mid-life point of the life cycle and enter the later years, they report that they have an emerging sense of the limited nature of time. They begin to measure life not by how far they have come, but by how much time they have left. They come to experience life as increasingly limited. In the second half of life the future feels as though it is narrowing; it seems that there are fewer possibilities, fewer options. It is no longer possible to do as much as we wanted to do in our youth. Now we must begin to choose. We must prioritize our goals. "I can't do it all. So what can I do?" asks the person in later years. "How best can I spend these years ahead of me?"

In theological terms this is the clinical experience of eschatology—the awareness of the shortness of the present time. Eschatology of course is built into the nature of life itself. Life will come to an end. Life is time-limited. In fact, each and every stage of life is time-limited. We often did not feel this sense of time-limitedness when we were youths or young adults. Life seemed more open then, more endless, more filled with possibilities. The problem then was selecting which possibility to do first. But in later life, we have a keener sense of the shortness of life in general and in particular of the shortness of our current life stage.

This awareness first emerges into our consciousness during the middle age years and then continues as a regular theme of the later years. Several researchers have noted that the theme of death, dying and destruction are present in the psyche of the mid-life person. Daniel J. Levinson, for example, who studied the stages of a man's growth writes:

> A man in the Mid-life Transition is troubled by his seemingly imminent death. He is beset even more by the anxiety that he will not be able to make his future better than his past. As he seeks to modify and enrich his life, he has self-doubts ranging in intensity from mild pessimism to utter panic: "Can I make my life more worthwhile in the remaining years? Am I now too old to make a fresh start? Have I become obsolete? What shall I try to do and be for myself, for my loved ones, for my tribe, for humanity?" The worst feeling of all is to contemplate long years of meaningless existence without youthful passions, creative effort or social contribution.[6]

Levinson has described so well the eschatological crisis. The awareness of death and the shortness of life raises questions of meaningfulness and worthwhileness. These questions lead people to reflect on and re-examine their lives and their goals. The dreams, illusions and plans of youth must be revised. In later life the individual may have to "let go" of some of the dreams of his or her youth. The youthful dreams must now be tempered with the realisms of the later years.

April always wanted to be a ballet dancer, but an early marriage, several children and odd working hours prevented all of that. When her daughters were old enough for lessons, however, she encouraged them to take ballet. The youngest seemed especially motivated. For many years April shared in and through her child's accomplishments. As she approached forty she began to be restless about her unfulfilled dream. "It's now or never," she thought. "I'll never be a ballerina at this point in my life, but I still want to learn, I still want to dance. What have I got to lose. I'm not getting any younger." So she enrolled in classes alongside her teenage daughter. In recent years the two of them have danced in several community productions separately and together. According to April, she has never been happier.

Life in the later years has this sense of eschtology about it, a keener awareness of the shortness of the present age. Some people respond to this awareness with despair. Others are motivated to redeem the time they have left and to make the most of it. The latter approach, which is more healthy psychologically and spiritually, is possible only if a person has grieved the loss of his youth.

Society's Pervasive Influence

Our experience of the loss of youth is influenced in large measure by social norms and attitudes. Being old is partially a social phenomenon. You are "old" when others tell you that you are old and you are still "young" if you behave the way others say a young person should behave.[7] Social roles and expectations are subtle pressures. I remember that during my younger years as a family therapist, I took pride in my ability to work effectively with adolescents. It seemed as though I could relate well to them, and many teens confirmed this self-perception during those years. Some ten or so years later, however, I remember being aware how much more often I seemed to side emotionally with the parents. I was sympathizing more with the parents' frustration than with the teen's rebellion. (It was no coincidence that I was a parent myself now.) Then one day it was confirmed. Susie was her name. She was a sixteen year old client who announced after the first session that she didn't like me as a counselor. She wanted someone her own age, someone who could understand her. I was put in my place—in more ways than one.

Each society defines "young" and "old" in its own terms and gives to these terms its own connotations. In American society "old" carries a negative connotation and "young" has a positive flavor. Old is considered obsolete, useless, out of date. Old appliances are thrown out. Old clothes are discarded. Old technology is not cost efficient and so it is replaced. This is a disposal society. When it gets old, throw it away. Little wonder then that older people feel as though they are being thrown away too. Their advice is not sought after. They are isolated from the mainstream of society. They are now useless, the "discards" of society.

America is a youth worshiping culture. The mass media reflects that. We love our young ideas, our fresh faces, our beautiful bodies. Progress has also been our collective idol. If it's new, it must be better. Yes, we worship progress. What we have not valued by comparison is maturity, tradition, roots, aged wisdom. Perhaps as the percentage of older people in the population increases, as it is expected to over the next fifty years, we will see a greater shift toward a more balanced picture of young and old. But for the moment, the connotations to the word "old" are still largely negative.

It also seems to be a well-established fact that there is in this society a kind of ageism, which Alex Comfort defines as "the notion that people cease to be people, cease to be the same people or become people of a distinct and inferior kind, by virtue of having lived a specific number of years. . . ."[8] This ageism, like its cousin racism, results in overt and covert acts of discrimination, bias and stereotyping. I suspect that ageism is the flip side of our society's obsession with youth. Both features, the ageism and the idolatry of youth, are products of our collective denial.[9] We deny the fact that we are aging. We deny the fact that we are no longer young. In countless hundreds of ways this society encourages that denial and we are all willing players in one form or another. How then is it possible for reasonable people to recognize, much less grieve, their loss of youth? At best it is difficult. At worst it never happens, and most people, when they finally realize that they are old, slip into a chronic state of despair and therein live out the remainder of their lives.

Finding New Meanings to "Old"

Ultimately, of course, "old" and "young" are not fixed commodities. There is no prescribed age that dictates when one is old.[10] Indeed, there are social pressures, but ultimately "old" and "young" are subjective experiences. We can be old way before our years and we can be "young in heart" way beyond our years. We have all known people in both camps. If we are to live healthy in our later years, we must transform the connotations attached to the word "old" and "young." We must, as Levinson says, "find positive meanings to being 'older' " and integrate the young and old within us. [11] Part of the grieving we do for our lost youth is a coming to terms with the word "old." Successful grieving will include an embracing and accepting of this word and a transforming of it into a positive image for us.

One of the barriers to this kind of transformation of the word "old" resides in the model of aging that most of us have in our minds. The prevailing model of aging is what is called the "Rise-Peak-Decline" model. This model, sometimes called the "low-high-low model," sees people growing throughout the first half of life and reaching a peak of development around mid-life and then spending the remainder of their lives in a long slow decline toward death. That's a pretty depressing view of the human journey! No wonder no one wants to enter the second half of life. There is some evidence to support this view, of course. Certainly in physical terms, we do grow, reach a peak, and then slowly decline. Yet, when we view humans from a wholistic perspective, we must agree with pastoral counselor William M. Clements that "The low-high-low scheme of viewing developmental reality is an illusion." [12] How do we account for such people as Winston Churchill, Albert Schweitzer, and Immanuel Kant, all of whom had their most productive and creative years late in life? Such people as these do not decline in later years. On the contrary, they continue to grow well into "old age" and probably right up to death's door. We might say that they end their lives at the peak of their spiritual development.

If we are to live the later years of our lives in psychological and spiritual health, we must revise our thinking about aging itself. We must realize that "the upward curve," as ethicist Charles E. Curran calls it, can and should continue throughout our entire life span. [13] We do not have to decline mentally or spiritually. On the contrary, we should look forward to old age the way we looked forward to our senior year of college, with anticipation and excitement for a period of time that will be the climax of our journey. [14] After many years of preparation, we are finally "going to put it all together." The later years of life can be a time of rich experience, deep relationships and spiritual maturity. If these years are to be such, however, we must transform the word "old" from a negative image into a positive one. Grieving our lost youth inevitably includes this kind of transforming.

Embracing the Present

The loss of youth is one of those necessary losses. We must deal with it and grieve it, if we are to go on with our lives, if we are to accept and even embrace who we are now. People have varieties of ways of coping or failing to cope with their loss of youth.

At age forty-three James was hardly an old man, but he felt like it. He was keenly aware of all of the little signs of aging. Each little change in his appearance panicked him. He didn't want to be old and didn't think that he had to be. So he worked out with weights, wore designer clothes, put a rinse on his hair, drove a sports car and delighted in the looks of the younger women at his office. His rationalization was, "Salesmen have to maintain an image, a young image. People don't want to deal with an old man." Maintaining his youth was linked with maintaining his job, thus giving even greater importance to the obsession to stay young.

From the vantage point of grief dynamics, James was denying the emerging loss of his youth. His feelings of sorrow frightened him. Too much of his worth and identity was tied up in being youthful. So he fled from his feelings, fled in the opposite direction, idolizing his lost youth. That worked well enough for a while, but with each passing year, James' defense mechanisms became all the more silly. By the time he was fifty-three years old, the tight pants and hip style wasn't cute. It was now getting pitiful. Instead of flirting with him, the younger women were now feeling sorry for him. Sex appeal turned to pity.

Let me suggest another version of a person denying their loss of youth, this time a female version.

Patty first came to me for marriage counseling. She had been married for close to seventeen years, but increasingly she felt bored with the relationship. She complained that there was no excitement, no passion, no romance in her life.

"Oh, he's a great guy," she would say, "and a great father, but I don't know if I really love him anymore. I love him, but I'm not in love with him. Do you know what I mean?"

"Not really," I responded. "Explain it to me."

"When we were younger and first in love, everything was exciting. He was so handsome, so sexy. We just couldn't stay away from each other. And we'd talk hours on end, sometimes until three in the morning. We just wanted to be together always."

"It sounds as though you are grieving for your lost youth, your lost romance."

"Sometimes I just want to run away," she continued. "I want to start over, maybe move up north. Make a new start. The kids can make it on their own. And Jack can easily find someone else. He's a good man. I have this deep urge to start over, before . . . "

"Before what?"

" . . . before it's too late."

The situation and feelings of Patty and James are so common that they are almost a caricature. Most counselors and clergy persons have talked with many people caught in these same dynamics. Both of these cases are in my view examples of individuals seeking to avoid facing their loss of youth. James feels it most sharply in terms of his appearance and physique. Patty feels it more in the relationship area where she longs for the lost romance of younger days. They both attempt to deny their loss in one form or another, to avoid their feelings and even flee from their own inner pain. James never seems to deal openly with his feelings and eventually becomes an object of pity not envy. Patty does deal more openly with her feelings and eventually works out her grief. Coupled with marital counseling, she is able to revitalize her marriage.

Theologically, I would suggest that both James and Patty have made youth into a false god. The god of youth is a very popular idol in America. There is plenty of encouragement for and money in the idolization of youth. James has lots of people wanting to sell him a product or a service that will help him deny his aging. Patty can wallow in soap operas and romance novels if she wants to worship at the altar of young love all day. Neither of them will grow psychologically or spiritually because of their allegiance to the god of youth. They will continue to believe that true happiness, i.e. salvation, lies in returning to the past, to something that is essentially lost.

Persons caught in this kind of idolatry are refusing psychologically to be the age they are. In a sense they are defying God's rule. God has made everything to age, everything that is alive. By refusing to mourn their youth, by refusing to even acknowledge the reality of loss, they are also refusing to accept God's reign. It is as if they are saying psychologically that "I am the creator, not God. I reject God's creation." They cannot imagine that life can be good in the future or even in the present. Salvation is found in going backward, not forward.

At age seventy-three Paul Tournier, the Swiss physician and popular Christian writer, was asked to reflect on aging and old age.[15] He believes that old age and retirement are "major problems in the world today," partly because we have put such a value on work and productivity. In reflecting on what constitutes successful aging, he focused in on the word "acceptance." If we are able to age well, he suggested, we must be able "to accept life in its entirety." Part of this acceptance, for Tournier, is accepting who and what we are at every stage of our life. He writes:

> To play the old man when one is young or the young man when one is old; to behave like a single person when one is married; to put on masculine manners when one is a woman; to affect love for a father whom one hates or to pretend to embrace when one is not—all this leaves behind it an ineradicable malaise, the feeling that one is in disharmony with oneself, with the truth about oneself. There is in the human heart a need for truth which one can indeed betray, but cannot get rid of.[16]

Tournier's words have much to offer those of us living through the later years of life. Acceptance means accepting the age or stage we are currently living through. It means being what we are. Acceptance is the opposite of denial. Denial rejects the present and wants the past. Acceptance embraces the present and looks forward to the future. This is indeed a good definition of faith or spiritual health, applicable to any age. The person of faith or maturity accepts life and his or her current life stage.

The loss of youth does not happen all at once. We tend to notice it first at mid-life, but the issue stays with us throughout the later years. The loss of youth is a gradual and persistent experience, and periodically over the years we will probably need to pause and identify this loss again and again. We will feel its pain most at marker events. At those times, we must, as Eugene C. Bianchi suggests,

> Seriously enter into the experience of the sands slipping away in the hour glass of our lives. This discomforting feeling of the unstoppable dimming of the light, the numbering of our breaths, *must be embraced until it hurts.*[17]

Grieving is indeed painful, but it is the only way to wholeness. So when those moments come, take time to grieve. Allow yourself some time and space to cry a little. For only in doing so can we again embrace the present.

As we discuss the other losses of the later years in future chapters, we would do well to remember this definition of mental and spiritual health as acceptance. We should not "borrow from the future" by living in fear of the next life stage. Neither should we live in the past by "idolizing" the life stage just completed. Live fully in the present. Enjoy it. Embrace it. Look for God there. However, in order to fully embrace the present, we must regularly let go of the past, and one of the most significant losses that we must periodically let go of is the loss of our youth.

Notes

1. Leo Missinne, geronotologist from the University of Nebraska, made the remark in a lecture given at Pilgram Place, Claremont, August 8, 1986.

2. I was first introduced to the term "marker event" in Bernice L. Neugarten's "Adult Personality: A Developmental View," *Human Development,* IX (1965), pp. 61–73.

3. The only socially prescribed marker event in later life is per-

haps retirement, but even here there are few commonly accepted rituals. I'll say more about this in Chapter Six.

4. The work experience of women is usually much different from that of men. Often women are just beginning a career in midlife, instead of plateauing out in one. I'll say more about this in later chapters. For the moment I just want to make the point that wrestling with career choices in later life is often a disguised way of wrestling with the loss of youth.

5. Judith Viorst, *Necessary Losses* (New York: Simon and Schuster, 1986), p. 269.

6. Daniel J. Levinson, *The Seasons of a Man's Life* (New York: Ballantine Books, 1976), p. 217.

7. Bernice L. Neugarten has done considerable work on the role of social norms in influencing when we complete certain life cycle events. She found that when people complete major developmental tasks is partly based on when they are expected to do so. See "Age Norms, Age Constraints and Adult Socialization," *American Journal of Sociology*, LXX (1965), pp. 710–17.

8. Alex Comfort, *A Good Age* (New York: Crown, 1976), p. 35.

9. Robert W. McClellan in his book *Claiming the Frontier: Ministry and Older People* (Los Angeles:University of Southern California, 1977) has introduced the term "gerontophobia," which is the "fear of aging." McClellan says this fear is a product of the collective denial of our own aging.

10. Perhaps one could argue that age sixty-five, set as it is by the federal government, is the age at which one is considered legally old. Psychologically some people feel old at forty; others don't consider themselves old until they are seventy-five.

11. Daniel J. Levinson, *The Seasons of a Man's Life*, p. 210.

12. William M. Clements, *Care and Counseling of the Aging* (Philadelphia: Fortress Press, 1979), p. 19. Bill has an interesting discussion of the whole low-high-low model of aging on pp. 19–22.

13. Charles E. Curran, "Aging: A Theological Perspective," in Carol LeFevre and Perry LeFevre, *Aging and the Human Spirit: A Reader in Religion and Gerontology*, second edition (Chicago: Exploration Press, 1981), p. 74.

14. Rabbi Abraham J. Herchel first introduced me to this image. He uses it in his "Older Person and the Family in the Perspec-

tive of Jewish Tradition," in Carol LeFevre and Perry LeFevre's *Aging and the Human Spirit,* ibid., pp. 35–44.

15. The result is *Learn To Grow Old* (New York: Harper and Row, 1972).

16. Ibid., pp. 184–85.

17. Eugene C. Bianchi, *Aging as a Spiritual Journey* (New York: Crossroad, 1982), p. 16. Emphasis is mine.

Chapter 4

The Loss of Family

"And his mother said to him, 'Son, why have you treated us so?' . . . And he said to them, 'How is it that you sought me? Did you not know that I must be in my Father's house?' " (Lk 2:48–49).

The middle years of adult life are spent building. We build a family, a career, a home and place in the community. It is a time for planting roots deep into the soil of our psyches. We build memories that last a lifetime. We form deep emotional attachments with one another. The latter half of life, however, is a time when what has been built up gradually dissolves. One by one (or, sometimes, all at once) we must let go of family, career and home. This chapter will focus on the loss of family, which begins as the children progressively become more autonomous, then independent and finally leave the family nest to lead their own lives and start their own families. Eventually, there are just the two of you again . . . or sometimes just one of you. This can be a difficult transition.

A Complexity of Emotions

I do not know too many parents who do not cognitively acknowledge that they want their children to be independent, autonomous adults. That is the general goal of all parenting. Emotionally, however, parents may have other feelings, some of them conscious, some of them unconscious, that influence how they handle the gradual loss of family. Emotionally, it may be hard to let go of children, because this loss involves so many other meanings.

- It may mean the end of my primary identity as parent.
- It may mean that I cannot control my children anymore, which in turn may mean that I am a failure.

- It may mean that my spouse and I no longer have any glue to hold us together.
- It may mean a deep sense of disappointment over how the children have turned out.
- It may mean that I cannot protect them from harm any longer and must risk their ultimate loss. And/or . . .
- It may mean that I am getting older and all of the implications therein.

Thus, the process of letting go of our children gets complicated. It may get contaminated with other issues and feelings. The grief is not pure.

Irene was a mother of three children altogether. The first two seemed to grow up reasonably well in spite of the divorce that split up the family. It helped that they were into their pre-teens by the time the family separated. But Jimmy was younger than the rest by about six years. He was Irene's baby, her desperate attempt to save the marriage by having a third child. Having Jimmy did not save the marriage, but it did create a strong and enmeshed bond between Irene and this child. Jimmy was six when his father left. From that point on Irene raised Jimmy alone as best she could. Jimmy was a handful to raise—a very bright child, a bit precocious, and he had a quick temper even from an early age. In addition Jimmy got used to being on his own, since his mother was gone a lot at work and on dates. She was always hoping to find Jimmy a father to replace the one that she blamed herself for "taking away." Jimmy of course never liked any of the men her mother brought home and made his views plain enough by his behavior.

As Jimmy grew older the conflicts between him and his mother intensified. Irene didn't like his smart mouth, his defiant attitude and his growing independence. She felt rejected by this child, "her baby" to whom she had given so much. Jimmy more or less ran wild in his early teens, and any attempt by Irene to put restrictions on him was met with outrage, defiance and running away behaviors. Jimmy was becoming a master at manipulating his mother, a situation that she allowed because she couldn't say "no."

Eventually Irene fell in love with another man and remarried, all of which necessitated that she move to another community to join her new mate. It seemed most appropriate at this time, given Jimmy's incorrigible behavior, to have him live with his natural father, who had by now also remarried. This would give Jimmy and his father time to get to know each other again. This arrangement worked for a while. Then Jimmy began to misbehave at dad's house too. When his father attempted to place restrictions on Jimmy, he would call his mother and "run away" to her house. She, of course, couldn't say "no" and would take him in. "Jimmy and I are so close . . . and he has had such a hard time of it," she would rationalize to herself. Sometime later Jimmy would miss his friends and go back to dad's. Jimmy went "back and forth" several times, playing one household against the other.

The issue reached crisis proportions when the local sheriff arrested Jimmy for selling drugs and the juvenile division officer recommended hospitalization for Jimmy for a brief period of time in order to get control of his behavior and his drug problem. Irene refused. "That's too drastic," she replied. "Jimmy is not that kind of kid. All he needs is love and attention." Irene couldn't or wouldn't face the reality that Jimmy had become a criminal, that Jimmy was out of control and that Jimmy had a drug problem. At a deeper level Irene was denying that Jimmy was "grown up," that she couldn't protect him any longer and that her "little boy" was gone. Irene's inability to "let go" actually prevented Jimmy from getting the help he needed. Eventually Jimmy ran afoul of the law again, and this time he was forced to get help through a period of confinement in a state youth camp.

My point in telling this story is to illustrate how complicated the process of letting go of one's children can be. Besides the obvious feelings of sorrow, there are many other issues that can get tangled up in the process, issues that usually have to do with the parent's needs and pathologies. Irene's difficulty in letting go of Jimmy expressed itself early in the way she failed to discipline the boy. She couldn't deal with the pain of loss, the pain of letting go of that last child, the last piece of her motherhood and family. When Irene attempted to say "no," Jimmy's defiance hooked her fear of losing him. Her difficulty was compounded by the false meanings she attached to this situation. It meant failure as a parent. Coupled with her perceived failure as a marriage partner, her self-worth couldn't risk another failure.[1] Because she could not deal with all this, she distorted the parent-child relationship, and her effectiveness as a parent was greatly diminished.

The Process Character of This Loss

The loss of family, like most losses in later life, is experienced as a gradual process. Actually parents can start losing their children, emotionally and socially, fairly early in life. In a sense parenthood is a lifelong process of "letting go." The process accelerates when the children move into the early adolescent period with its natural surge toward autonomy. Increasingly children in this period move away from dependency. They start making some of their own decisions without relying on or consulting with their parents. They start valuing the opinions of peers more than those of their parents. All the signs are there, if we notice them.

Do you remember how you felt when your young teenage daughter first kept a secret from you? The locked diary? The secret letter to a friend at camp? Now there is a part of her life that you do not share. Some parents find this secrecy threatening. Others ride with it as natural development. Remember, too, the time, perhaps a little later, when your son first decided that attending a family event wasn't as important to him as attending an event with his friends? He chose peers over family. How did you feel? Did you allow his decision or enforce your will that he go with the family? It is hard to know how much freedom to allow a young adult without losing family unity. Embedded in this issue is how you, as a parent, feel about the growing distance between you and your child.

As teenagers grow older into late adolescence, their independence grows as well. Now they are literally gone more. Perhaps they drive now and so they spend more time away from home. More and more they manage their own money, choose their own clothes, select their own friends, form their own priorities. In addition, the culture fosters the growing distance between teenager and parents by creating a teen subculture. The youth culture has its own fashions, its own language and its own music, all of which reinforces the adolescent's natural urge to be different, to be autonomous. At times it seems as though our children are becoming a different species. We don't recognize them, much less communicate with them. That's frustrating and frightening. We want them to be "like us," but we also want them to be their own person. Which side of this dilemma do we push?

Many parents do not encourage autonomy in their children. They experience their adolescent's emerging autonomy as a "losing." They cannot deal with the feelings of loss, so they resist the change in subtle and not so subtle ways. All of this makes "leaving home" a much more difficult and even traumatic experience for the family than it might otherwise have been, and in some tragic cases causes a bitterness between parent and child that is never repaired. Psychiatrist Roger L. Gould reminds us of the inevitability of growth when he writes:

> If we "stonewall" against changing and insist that our main role is to be their parents, we can force their changes into less healthy but nevertheless necessary expression. Like the flow of a powerful river, the need to grow can only be diverted, never totally dammed.[2]

Other parents of course do encourage autonomy in their teenage children. Such parents have prepared themselves well for the eventual loss of family and accept its gradual coming with grace and patience. Such parents, in my view, have done their grief work. They have faced their own feelings, and by so doing they are better able to pass through this transition and better able to facilitate their children's passage. Autonomy comes gradually, and so grieving should come gradually as well. If autonomy and "letting go" both occur in parallel steps, then each step toward autonomy will be one that both parent and child are ready for.[3]

For Christian parents the task can be both more difficult and filled with more resources. Pastoral theologian Herbert Anderson comments on the nature of love and parenthood for Christians when he says,

> The process of leaving home is often as painful as it is necessary. . . . For parents, the fundamental task is to act out

the conviction that loving means letting go. The parental love that lets go and sends children forth to serve in the world parallels the love of God in Christ. For Christian parents, baptism has been a sign from the beginning that our children already belong to God.[4]

Remembering that our children belong to God is a helpful barrier against "making idols" out of our children or out of the nuclear family. It is also a way of encouraging us to grieve "in advance" the eventual loss of our children as children. We must always remember that our children will not be children forever. Yet, effective parents are not just those who grieve well, but those who know how to balance loving and grieving, holding close and letting loose, restricting and liberating. Both elements are important.

Ambivalent Feelings

What should be painfully clear is that the loss of family involves some ambivalent feelings for the adult parents. Like few other losses, the loss of family carries a mixture of positive and negative feelings. Talking to parents who are largely through this transition reveals the primacy of the feelings of nostalgia and relief.

I was sitting with Harold and Jane Walter who were sharing with me some of their feelings now that their child-rearing years are largely over. I asked them to show me their family albums in which they have pictures of their children from birth on. Most parents have one or several of these albums filled with pictures. As we thumbed through the pages, I could tell that the pictures brought back memories—wonderful memories. Often a particular picture would trigger a story or two. Remember the time that . . .

. . . Susan first learned to ride a bicycle. I can still see you holding on to the rear seat, running along beside her, as she wobbled down the sidewalk.

. . . We bought a puppy for Daniel's fourth birthday. We hid it in the laundry room overnight and it cried like a baby. You ended up sleeping with it.

. . . I was so scared when Susy first started driving on her own.

Gosh, we thought for sure we would hear from the police or the hospital within the hour.

. . . Danny was in that hiking accident and we spent all night at the hospital, waiting to see if he was going to pull through. And what did he say when he woke up: "Where's the ice cream?"

. . . You coached Brandon's little league team one year. Now that was an experience! The screaming parents. The innocent kids. And the day that Brandon hit the home run that won the game. Those were great years.

. . . Remember how Susan looked on her wedding day. How beautiful. How grown up. I will never forget that day as long as I live. Let me show you Susy's wedding pictures. . . . [5]

Almost every parent has memories like these. It is not too hard to get most post-parenting couples to talk about their memories of their family years. Even the trying times and the scary times don't seem so bad in the perspective of the later years. Even the rough years seem wonderful. Most people can easily identify their feelings of nostalgia for the family years.

Almost within the same breath and certainly within the same conversation, the Walters also talked about their feelings of relief. I asked them, "Would you do it again? Would you like to have a family back—perhaps another child?"

"Nope, not on your life!" they announced. "Too much responsibility. Too much worry. We are too old for that now. God was wise to give children to younger parents. You have the energy for them then, and the time and the patience. Now it's a relief just to have them grown up."

Jane Walter was especially thankful not to have children around. "Those were great years," she said, "but since then I have developed my own flower shop. The shop has been something that I always wanted to do. I began it when Brandon was still in high school and now it's going great guns. I wouldn't have time for a family now, even if I wanted one—and I don't." Many women can resonate with Mrs. Walter's feelings. It's nice having the free time that the empty nest years allow. Now there is time to develop a career, or travel, or enjoy that often neglected hobby.

Most of us can identify with these two common emotions: nostalgia and relief. Other post-parenting adults may have stronger, more extreme versions of these emotions. They may long deeply for the lost family and correspondingly don't feel very positive about the empty nest years. They still live in and through the lives of their children. Perhaps they interfere with the lives of their adult children. Perhaps they are still trying to be mother or father—still trying to control, still trying to be needed. That's it. The feeling is one of not being needed anymore. That's the painful feeling . . . not being needed anymore.

On the other extreme some parents may have bitter feelings about their children's departure. Perhaps their children did not turn out so well. They are not only relieved that parenting is over, but angry and resentful that it didn't turn out better. They feel that their children "owe" them more—more respect, more help, more something. "The children just took, took, took," they complain, "and never, not once, said thank you." Have you met such parents?

The feelings we have around the loss of family can be and usually are very ambivalent. They certainly include nostalgia and relief. And in some individuals they can even take more extreme forms, forms that signify unresolved grief.

The Wounded Parent

We all have dreams for our children. We want them to be happy, well adjusted. We dream that they will be someone important. We dream of their careers, their marriages, their accomplishments. Sometimes we dream dreams for them that are really our unfulfilled dreams.[6] We live our lives over again in them. That is dangerous. We also have the more specific expectations for our children. We expect them to follow our morals, our family standards, our dictates regarding grades, behavior and the like. What happens when they do not fulfill our dreams or follow our expectations? In fact, they reject our wishes in large part. There can be a kind of loss there that is powerful and painful.

Betty and Bob Molberg were very religious people. Bob had been raised in a Christian home with a strict moral code. Betty had been raised in a broken home, but wanted to do better by her children. They thought that they had given their oldest daughter Mary everything that a child could want or need. This included not only material things, but also affection, family stability and proper religious training. It seemed as though Mary flowered in this environment. She was a nice, well-behaved child who never did much without consulting with her parents. In her teens she became more independent than her age merited, but her parents had always trusted her. Actually there were lots of signs of trouble, but her parents did not see them then. So it really came as a shock to them when she ran away from home the summer before her senior year in high school.

The Molbergs found out two days later that Tom, an eighteen year old recent high school graduate, also had "left home." And they found out from Tom's stepfather that Mary and Tom had been "going together" for the past six months. That was the real shocker! Why did she hide this from them? What else might be going on? Their minds imagined the worst. Bob's shock turned to anger: "How could she do this to us?" He wanted to disown his daughter on the spot. Betty's reaction was more guilt oriented: "What did I do wrong? Why didn't she come to us? Why won't she contact us now?"

The Molbergs heard from Mary some time later. She was living with Tom on a ranch of sorts in a nearby state. Bob wanted to go there immediately and force her to come home, but Mary threatened to run away farther away if he came after her. The parents could do nothing but wait. Conversations by telephone and letters occurred and piece by piece more of the story unfolded of how Mary fell "in love" with Tom but couldn't confide in her parents who she knew would disapprove of him; of how she felt alienated from church and the family's moral code; and of how she just wanted to "have fun" and "be on her own" for a while. The Molbergs felt rejected by their daughter's communications. Their frustration turned to anger and depression. They felt helpless. For the first time in their life Mary was out of their sight, out of their reach—to both control and to aid. They were afraid and angry.

Four months passed. Bob and Betty had their hands full trying to explain this situation to their younger children, to Mary's church friends and to the extended family. It was a painful time. Increasingly in conversations that Betty had with her daughter (Bob refused to talk to her), she felt that there was more to the story than what was being said. Betty reflected that Mary sounded more unsure of herself in recent weeks. This weighed heavily on the Molbergs. Then one Saturday Bob announced that he had had enough of this and decided to take matters into his own hands. He drove all day and night to the place where he suspected Mary to be. Upon his arrival he found Mary living in a commune type arrangement, but there was no Tom to be found. He had recently left, but not without leaving his mark—Mary was eight months pregnant. Bob was able to persuade his daughter to come home with him, at least for the baby's sake.

Mary's attitude toward her parents did not improve much at home. She was hostile toward them and resented their attempts to help her as ploys to make her stay home, "like I was a little kid or something." The Molbergs couldn't understand why Mary resented them so much. They were "only trying to help." Fortunately, they were able to get Mary into some counseling and eventually that personal counseling evolved into family therapy. This process helped all of the Molbergs coexist during the period of the baby's birth.

The relationship between Mary and her parents never really improved until years later. And today, some ten years later, they all agree that they have an excellent relationship. The key factors that facilitated the healing of this relationship was Mary's experience of being a mother herself and her parents coming to terms with their own feelings of loss and resentment toward their daughter. Concerning this latter point, the Molbergs continued in counseling long after Mary had dropped out. Their primary task during this period of counseling was to work on the terrible sense of loss that they felt about Mary. To them Mary had "thrown her life away." She was given everything and gave it up for a pig's den. The Molbergs couldn't understand it or accept it. They had such wonderful dreams for Mary. She could have been anything she wanted—a doctor, a missionary, a teacher—but all that was gone now. They were forced to grieve for the loss of their idealized daughter, the daughter that might have been.

Variations on the Theme

These are times in which the "normal" or typical nuclear family has given way to various other types of family constellations. We now have more single parent families, more serial marriages, more childless couples, and so on. What all of this means is that there are many possible variations on the theme of loss of family. The experience of the loss of family can come to people in differing shapes and forms. Let's look at some examples.

Donna is currently a sixty-four year old single woman, who has always been on the timid, dependent side of the spectrum. Her husband walked out on her some twenty years earlier, but her four children have continued to be involved in her life. Two of the children continued to live with her in the family home well into their twenties. Then one of the older girls, following her divorce, moved back in with "Mom," bringing her little two year old with her. Donna has not experienced the loss of her family yet. She has never really been without children in the home. She has always been "Mom" in one form or another. She probably will not really go through this transition until she is almost seventy and then it will probably be a welcomed relief.

Melvin was a father of four children, ages eight to sixteen, when he and his wife divorced. It was a very bitter divorce, in part because Linda quickly remarried the man that she had been having an affair with during her marriage with Melvin. All four children decided to remain living with their mother in the family home with the new stepfather. Melvin tried to keep up with the visitations with his children as regularly as he could, but over the years that followed his visitations grew more infrequent. The older children had busy schedules that left little time for dad, and Mel's company began to ask him to travel more often (partly because they knew that he was unencumbered with family now). Six years passed. Melvin became more dissatisfied with his life. He was depressed and very lonely in spite of his girlfriend's affection. He could never pinpoint the problem until his oldest daughter got married and he had to be out of town. Then he began to realize how much he had missed out on during the past few years. He wasn't there to see Paul drive or see Esther's first date or Timmy's soccer games. He missed all that. He had been cheated out of fatherhood. Mel's loss of family was very painful.

Jerry had two families. His first marriage was early in his life and resulted in four children. His wife died of cancer when the children were approaching young adulthood. He coped as a single parent for five years, seeing the oldest two children through high school. It was hard to get over the death of his wife, and in spite of a modest social life, he never got serious about anyone. His wife was still there in the faces and mannerisms of the two oldest girls. As they finished high school and one went to college and the other got married, it was almost as though he was losing Michelle (his wife) all over again. Yet, it also freed him up in a way. He did get serious after that about a woman who was twelve years his junior. Elizabeth and he soon married and she brought one child to this new marriage. Jerry and Elizabeth then had a baby of their own within the year. Now the household included "mine, yours and ours." About the time that Jerry finished with one family, he started another one. His experience of the loss of family was prolonged and double barreled.

What becomes clear from these sample vignettes is that "family" means more than the mere presence of children. Family means everything we associate with home and family life. When we lose family, we lose a home, an identity, and, maybe most of all, a way of life.[7] The loss of family includes all of these related losses. The other thing that is clear from these "variations" is that the loss of family can come to us in many different ways. There is no set time or stage of life in which one loses the family. Some people can experience this loss early in life, others late in life, and still others continuously as one family is replaced by another.

The Physiological Component

The loss of family, as described in this book, is primarily a social-psychological process. However for women there is also a clear physical change that is associated with the loss of family. That physical change is of course menopause. Menopause is the time when a woman ceases to go through the monthly reproductive cycle. For her it is the loss of fertility, the final realization that one will never be a mother again.[8] For some women this is a welcomed relief. They are glad to be done with the inconvenience and discomfort of menstrual cycles. For others it is experienced as an intensification of what they are already experiencing interpersonally—the loss of children. Again we note the presence of the two emotions, relief and nostalgia. These two are the most common emotions associated with the loss of family.

It is interesting to observe that menopause is often referred to as "the change of life." This popular description of menopause is filled with more truth than we might otherwise admit. For there is more changing here than just a woman's bio-chemistry. Often at about the same time, a woman is also dealing with the passage of her children from childhood to adulthood and correspondingly the passage of her role from mother to friend. The physiological process and the interpersonal process may mirror each other. With this "change of life," the adult woman enters a new life stage filled with new potentials and new possibilities.

New Possibilities

The stage of adult life that is post-child rearing has been labeled by many writers as the empty nest period. This period of our lives refers to the interval in a couple's life between the time that the last child leaves home and a first spouse dies. As we view the human life cycle from an historical perspective, we note that this stage of life has actually increased in length with the advent of better health habits and modern medical procedures. Thomas B. Robb, writing in *The Bonus Years,* notes that the older couple today will spend two-thirds as much time in the period after completion of child rearing as they did in child rearing. In 1890 the death of the first spouse occurred on average two years *before* the completion of the parental role, whereas in 1950 this event occurred an average of fourteen years *after* the end of the child rearing period.[9] What this means of course is that we have more time than ever before in this empty nest period. It is a period when the home is probably empty of children, at least our immediate children. The heavy responsibilities of parenthood are probably finished. There is probably more money available now than ever before in our lives. Hopefully there are no limiting health problems yet to deal with. This stage of life, then, can be one of the most creative, productive and stable in an individual's and couple's life.

Erik Erikson has written much on the seventh stage of the human life cycle, called Generativity. In this stage mature adults move toward investing themselves in caring for the next generation. The immature or developmentally arrested adult "stagnates." Caring is the chief virtue to flower in mature adults and it is expressed in their desire to invest themselves in people and causes larger than themselves.[10] Pastoral theologian Don S. Browning has suggested that this Generativity stage, if the crisis is resolved positively, is the zenith of the Christian journey.[11] This stage of life offers the clearest potential for the individual to become spiritually mature and in a sense is the goal toward which the Christian journey moves.

Generativity is of course more than having children, although that can be one expression of it. Generativity is broader than raising children, and this "stage" includes both the late child rearing years and the empty nest years. As we move into the empty nest period, our generative desires should take the form of caring for the larger community, for the earth, for the generations to follow. Yet we cannot invest ourselves in such "carings" if we are still stuck in the throws of an aborted grief process for our own family. Getting to this empty nest period is not easy. It involves passing through the loss of our family.

Robert C. Peck, who has specialized in the study of the personality of older adults, has attempted to describe the psychological changes that need to occur in the individual if that individual is to pass through the later years of life in psychological health. In that regard he has introduced the term "cathectic flexibility," which is one crucial feature of successful aging. Cathectic flexibility is a type of "emotional flexibility: the capacity to shift emotional investments from one person to another, and from one activity to another."[12] Peck argues that as we enter the later years, we must develop this ability to let go of emotional investments that are gone and reinvest ourselves in new attachments if we wish to age well. Translated: one must learn to grieve well. The opposite of this, cathectic impoverishment, occurs when a person gradually loses love objects (as we inevitably do in later life) and does not replace them with new attachments. Gradually then the person becomes more and more emotionally impoverished. There are fewer and fewer "things" that the person cares about, and without caring the older person eventually stagnates.

This concept can obviously apply to any and all of the losses during the later years of life. However, nowhere is it more applicable than as it pertains to the loss of family and the transition into the "creative years."[13] Persons who can be flexible, "letting go" of children and their parental roles, are then able to form new attachments during the empty nest period, new attachments that will enrich this period of their lives. Others who are emotionally rigid cannot let go and will remain stuck in the earlier stage of life, never to find the full potential of the empty nest period. How well the loss of family is handled then significantly colors how creative or uncreative the empty nest period really is.

From Children to Friends

Unlike many other losses of later life, the loss of family offers us a wonderful opportunity for a new relationship with our adult children. Many post-parental adults speak fondly of the relationship they now have with their adult children, relationships described often as friendships. Such relationships are not possible until the loss of family experience is passed through, by both parents and children.

Many parents see their children as extensions of themselves, or as their possessions, or as the fulfillment of their unfulfilled lives. These are all potentially destructive attitudes to have toward raising one's children. All of these "beliefs" make children into "little idols" in one form or another. We "idolize" them. We hallow them and their achievements. We have to, because we have invested so much of ourselves in them. Such idolatry, created by unresolved grief, not only blocks grieving, but blocks the opportunity to discover our children as adults.

The central theological question is: Whom do our children belong to? For people of faith, the answer should be: God. Isn't that what we acknowledge in infant baptism or dedication? God gives them to us as gifts. They are on loan. Our job is to raise them, teach them, love them and then launch them into the world, thereby returning them to God. They are with us only for a short time. One of my favorite passages that reflects this non-possessive attitude toward children is Kahlil Gibran's poem which reads:

Your children are not your children.
They are the sons and daughters of Life's longing for itself.

They come through you but not from you,
And though they are with you yet they belong not to you.

You may give them your love but not your thoughts,
For they have their own thoughts.
You may house their bodies but not their souls,
For their souls dwell in the house of tomorrow, which you
    cannot visit, not even in your dreams.

You may strive to be like them, but seek not to make them
    like you.
For life goes not backward nor tarries with yesterday.
You are the bows from which your children as living arrows
    are sent forth.
The archer sees the mark upon the path of the infinite, and
    He bends you with His might that His arrows may go
    swift and far.
Let your bending in the Archer's hand be for gladness;
For even as He loves the arrow that flies, so He loves also the
    bow that is stable. [14]

One of the things that helps parents avoid making idols out of
their children or related false gods is having other concerns and
causes in their lives. Children are only a part of their parents' lives,
not all of it. When parents start making the part into the whole, they
have essentially created a idol. This is why it is a wise piece of advice
in parenting to save time and energy to focus on other concerns.
Have a career. Develop interests outside of the home. Invest yourself in your marriage. This kind of a more balanced style of parenting
actually helps the children. They benefit from being with parents
who are truly alive. They also benefit from not feeling so much pressure to be everything for their parents, to fulfill their unlived lives,
to bolster their shaky egos. It is difficult for children to leave home
psychologically and physically when they are "needed."

If we work through the loss of family in a reasonable and timely
fashion, there is great potential for new possibilities with these
unique individuals we call "children." If we can let go of our children
as children, we create the possibility of relating to them as adults,

even friends. Few other losses in later life have this built-in potential. Not everyone is able to have an adult relationship with his or her children. There are many variables, some of which are out of our control. We are blessed if this kind of relationship occurs. But it will only emerge, even if only as a possibility, if we let go of our children as children. Only then can we see them and ourselves as individuals. New life will emerge out of old, but only if we pass through the transition called the loss of family.

Notes

1. Reflect for a moment: What is the hidden idol being worshiped here?

2. Roger L. Gould, *Transformations: Growth and Change in the Adult Life* (New York: Simon and Schuster, 1978), p. 225.

3. Many of the problems that families with adolescents have can be summarized as poor timing: either the child wants more independence than the parents are ready to give or the parents give the child more freedom than the teenager is ready to handle. In either case conflicts emerge. Grief or our readiness to let go is thus an underlying issue in effective parenting.

4. Herbert Anderson, *The Family and Pastoral Care* (Philadelphia: Fortress Press, 1984), pp. 63–64.

5. The ritual that comes closest to being a marker event for the loss of family is the wedding of one of the parents' children. Often in the midst of this ritual, the parents grieve the loss of their daughter or son and in a larger sense the loss of their family. Clergy would do well to be aware of this dimension to the wedding ceremony.

6. You can see clearly how the loss of family and the loss of youth can be entangled in some adults. Actually, all of these losses are interrelated and can mutually reinforce or block each other's grief.

7. The loss of a home is often associated with the loss of family. Many post-parenting couples, for example, relocate to smaller more manageable quarters after the children leave home.

8. The male version of this loss of fertility is not nearly so encompassing or complex. Nevertheless, some men will have feelings of grief associated with a vasectomy.

9. Thomas Bradley Robb, *The Bonus Years: Foundations for Ministry with Older Persons* (Valley Forge: The Judson Press, 1968), p. 64. Emphasis is mine.

10. Levinson's version of this same dynamic is captured in the word "legacy." He says that the mid-life man is concerned with legacy and that this concern can take many forms, including children, passing on material possessions and/or creating work that will transcend him. See *Seasons of a Man's Life*, pp. 219ff.

11. See Don S. Browning, *Generative Man: Psychoanalytic Perspectives* (Philadelphia: Westminster Press, 1973).

12. Robert C. Peck, "Psychological Developments in the Second Half of Life," in Bernice L. Neugarten, *Middle Age and Aging*, p. 89.

13. Reuel L. Howe first used the phrase "creative years" to describe this stage of life in the 1950's. See his *The Creative Years* (Greenwich, CT: Seabury Press, 1959).

14. Kahlil Gibran, *The Prophet* (New York: Alfred A. Knopf, 1923), pp. 21–22.

Chapter 5

The Loss of Parents

"Honor your father and your mother, that your days may be long in the land which the Lord your God gives you" (Ex 20:12).

All of us have parents. Our parents gave us life. They cared for us when we were helpless. They raised us. They molded and shaped our personalities for better or worse. When we were younger we feared losing our parents. That was the most frightening nightmare we could imagine. That primal fear never really goes away. In the second half of life most all of us will realize that fear. We will live to bury one and probably both of our parents.

The Aging Parent

It is no secret that the population of the United States is changing and becoming more "gray." The birth rate is declining, but, more importantly for our purposes, the length of life is extending. The life expectancy figures are now up to 78.4 and 82.6 years for men and women respectively, an increase in approximately nine percent in this century.[1] The combination of these factors means that the percentage of older people in the population is increasing and the trend is expected to continue well into the twenty-first century.[2] Most of us can relate to this larger cultural trend in very personal ways. Most of us have or will have parents that will live or are living well into their eighties or longer. The second half of life is inevitably filled with the issues and reactions to the aging and eventual death of our parents.

Sometimes the middle generation (ages thirty to sixty years) is called the "sandwich generation," because it is "caught in the middle" between the demands of aging parents and the responsibilities of growing children. This current generation of adult children is probably feeling the full impact of this squeeze more than any other generation prior to it. The declining birth rate, for example, means that there are fewer adult children available today to support and care for aging parents. In addition the increased employment of women outside of the home means that women, who are traditionally the care-givers, are less available to care for aging parents than have been their mothers and grandmothers.[3] All this goes to make this generation of adult children feel more "caught" than most. Given the trends in the population, the prospects for the future do not appear to be much different than what this generation is currently experiencing.[4]

Another social trend that impacts our relationships with our aging parents is the general mobility of our society. We are a very mobile people compared to other cultures and nations. It is not uncommon for parents and their adult children to live in distant towns or even states. In previous centuries this was not the case. Sometimes two, three or four generations of a family were all to be found living within a few miles of each other. This is still the pattern in many rural communities, but increasingly the norm is becoming more one of parents living in a separate residence from their children, residences that may be in a distant town, city or even state.[5] Telecommunications and affordable travel alleviate some of the effects of this distance. Most of us do talk with our parents regularly, but rarely do we see them on a daily basis.

The third cultural factor that impacts our personal relationships with our parents as they age is the cultural isolation of the elderly. As people enter "old age," whenever that is, they progressively move out of the mainstream of society into specialized facilities designed to meet their unique needs for socialization, health care and the like. These facilities can include "homes" for the aged scattered throughout the community or whole "villages" devoted to serving the elderly. Eventually, when our parents' health declines even further, they will probably relocate again to a hospital, a hospice, or a convalescent facility. There is great convenience and wisdom in the trend toward specialized facilities for the elderly. There are also several disadvantages. Chief among them is the isolation of the elderly from day to day contacts and interaction with people of other generations. We and our parents both are poorer for it.

All of these cultural trends combine to make it easy for us to avoid emotional involvement with our aging parents. They are not aging before our eyes, so to speak. We do not have to think about them very much. "Out of sight, out of mind," as the saying goes. The needs of the elderly, and in particular the needs of our parents, can easily get placed on the back burner of life. Some of this avoidance can be attributed to physical circumstances, but some of it is also an expression of our own denial mechanisms. We don't want to think about our parents getting older. We don't want to deal with their loss, and yet, even in the present moment, we are gradually losing them. Because our society has so successfully isolated the elderly, we can conveniently avoid them and our feelings about that impending loss. Our denial is made easy.

Denial can be a two-way street. Many aging parents do not want to see themselves as aging. They can contribute to the collective denial by reassuring us when we phone periodically that "everything is fine here." Do you have a father who doesn't tell you when he went in for surgery until after its over? Doesn't he say, "I didn't want to worry the kids"? Our parents don't want to be a burden or a bother to anyone, especially to their children. Most older people hate having to ask for help and they would certainly rather not be an object of pity. So, they too may avoid facing their own gradual aging and decline in physical well-being. And if we, their adult children, are also trying to avoid facing reality, the end result can be a kind of collusion of denial. With this kind of collusion operating, it is easy to avoid dealing with our aging and eventually dying parents until it's too late to do much constructively.

Aging Brings Changes

As our parents age there are several subtle changes that occur in their psychology and in their interpersonal relationships with their adult children. These changes signal to us that we are losing them as parents, that they are declining in health, influence and energy.

How we respond to these changes reflects our willingness to deal with our own feelings of loss and anxiety.

There has been considerable discussion in the literature on aging that describes the increasing dependency that older people experience as they age after sixty-five.[6] That dependency takes many forms. With health limitations, they need more assistance with the daily routines of shopping, washing clothes, banking, etc. With a limited income, they may need financial support from their adult children. And with decreasing energy, they must move to smaller quarters and eventually to a health care facility. The dependency is also psychological. Older people, particularly single people, are lonely. They need to socialize and they enjoy talking about family and the past. If our single parent lives in isolation, then he or she can become especially dependent on us.

"Every time I call Mama," says Yolanda, "she sounds so pathetic and lonely. She could talk my ear off all day, if I let her. And it's usually about old times or about the lousy job that her cleaning lady does or how the mailman messed up her mail. She always ends the conversation with, 'When are you coming to see me?' "

The corresponding concept that is frequently mentioned in the aging literature is "role reversal." As our parents age, adult children experience a gradual reversal of the roles. Our parents become more dependent, more child-like, and we become more parent-like, supportive and nurturing of them. We begin to "parent our parents." We may start to make decisions for them, give them advice, and in some cases literally care for their physical needs, even as they cared for us when we were but infants in their arms.

Bruce, a middle-age child of an ailing parent, for example, told me that his mother got so she wouldn't take her medicine until he scolded her about its importance. "At first," said Bruce, "it felt weird, scolding my mother. She certainly gave me hell many times over the years, but then I began to realize that it really wasn't a matter of who's the parent or child, it's part of our family habit. That's how mother knows that I love her. That's how she loved me. She wants me to scold her." So Bruce continued scolding his mother quite regularly until the end, and when she did die several years later, he scolded her for that too.

What these subtle changes in roles and psychology suggest is that we begin to lose our parents as parents long before they actually die. Our parents cease to function as parents as they decline in health and energy. We begin to feel that they are not the tower of strength, wisdom and nurture that they have always been—or at least that is how they seemed. We must be willing to allow our parents and our relationship with our parents to change. Some adult children of aging parents cannot do that. It's too frightening to let go of the image of their parents as strong, independent, available people. I would suggest that such people have made "little idols" of their parents or a particular image of their parents. They cannot see their parents as individuals. They cannot allow their parents to change, because it shatters their rigid role definitions and subtle idolization.

It is hard to watch one's parents age. It is hard to see their health deteriorate, to see them lose their love of life, to watch them narrow their lives and give up cherished goals. It may be hard, too, to deal with their dependency needs and the subtle role reversal that occurs. It is hard to see all of this happen in people whom we once so admired or feared or both. How will we respond to these changes? Can we deal with our own feelings of loss, so that we can accept the changes that are occurring and respond to our parents with kindness? Or will we hide behind our denial systems and avoid contact with them, continuing to force them to be someone they are not in order to keep our idolatrous images intact? As our parents age, we do experience the first glimpses of their loss and respond accordingly.

As hard as it is to deal with our aging parents and their eventual deaths, there is a strong thrust in western religious traditions toward caring for the elderly and in particular for one's parents. To some extent this tradition has been weakened by the forces of modern society, including secularism, mobility and the isolation of age groups. Our ability to care for our aging parents is directly related to our willingness to face our own grief feelings about the emerging loss of our parents. Because we deny our own painful feelings of loss, we avoid, ignore, do not respect and sometimes even ridicule our elderly parents. God wants us to care for the aging, but in order to do so, we must face our grief openly.

Did you ever notice that there is a conditional clause in the fifth commandment, "Honor your father and mother . . . "? The rest of the imperative reads, " . . . that your days may be long in the land the Lord God gives you." There is something about honoring our parents that will enable us to live long lives ourselves. That's a bit strange. Most people would think the opposite, that they might have less stress, and therefore live longer, if they ignore their aging parents. Yet, the commandment clearly implies that our ability to live long lives is dependent upon whether or not we honor our own parents. Catholic priest and professor of gerontology Leo Missinne has suggested that the meaning of this commandment is that the more we are involved with our own aged parents, the more we are preparing ourselves for our own aging.[7] Our parents are our future. Where they are now is where we shall be someday. We will cope better with our old age if we are involved with caring for our aging parents now.

The Slow Death

Death can come in varied forms and manners, but the long slow death is one of the hardest to handle. Modern medicine and hospitals being what they are, most of our parents will die in hospitals or nursing homes and most of them will have protracted dying processes. In contrast to the sudden death, the slow death allows us time to anticipate our parents' death. We are able to prepare ourselves for the unwelcomed event. Yet if the dying becomes too long or too filled with suffering, we may come to the point where we start wanting our parents to die. Death can be a blessing for those who have suffered long. It can also come as a release for the adult child, a release from the long vigil.

The hardest thing for the adult child about these kinds of dyings is the emotional drain. Long terminal illnesses may involve several periods of hospitalization and eventually a longer stay in a nursing home and then, finally, death—or maybe even another brief recovery, followed by another round of illness. These are difficult situations. They are emotionally exhausting. It is as if we start and stop our own grief process again and again. Each time there is a crisis, we begin again to prepare ourselves emotionally to deal with the final loss of our parent. Then when our parent rallies, our grief is put "on hold," only to be reactivated when the next crisis comes along. The emotional roller-coaster of a chronic illness is taxing on all.[8]

Our parents of course would rather avoid such circumstances too. Most older people would rather die quickly than be a prolonged financial and emotional burden upon their families. Some families, therefore, try to decide in advance how they will handle slow deaths. Once our time comes, however, the situation becomes a different matter altogether. Now it is *our* mother in that hospital bed or *our* father in the nursing home. It is no longer a hypothetical example. We feel obligated to do everything possible to make mom comfortable or to give dad every chance of recovery. It is not something that we can treat casually or intellectually. It's an emotional time.[9]

At the start of a parent's critical illness it may not be clear to us what we're dealing with, whether this is the end or just the beginning of a long decline. We do not know whether we are in for a sprint or a marathon. Initially, we drop what we are doing and rush to his or her side. But then the illness drags on and on, and at some point we must shift gears psychologically from a crisis mentality into a "long haul" mentality. That is hard. Somewhere in the middle of our current busy schedule, we must now fit time for an ill parent, either in person or by phone or by semi-regular trips. Inevitably the people that get short-changed are our spouse and children. Sometimes they come to resent our increased involvement, physically and emotionally, with our ill parent. Old family jealousies surface. Now we have even more stress to deal with—trying to care for the ill parent and trying to keep the spouse and children off our backs. All of this can and does impact how we handle the slow death of an aging parent. Little wonder that when mom or dad does "pass on," we feel a sense of relief—for them and for ourselves.

When Jean returned from burying her ninety-two year old mother, she was more relieved than sorrowful. "Mother had been ill so long," she said, "and suffered so long. I think that she wanted to go at the end. She just waved people off. She wouldn't take her pills or cooperate with the nurses. I think she wanted to die at that point—and who can blame her." Because of this situation Jean's grieving process was different. There was more relief in her grief. There was more of a mixture of gratitude and sorrow. Several weeks after her mother's death, she said: "It's not as bad as I thought it would be. I thought I would be devastated when Mom died, but it's manageable. Oh, sure I miss her, but it's not the way I felt after dad's

sudden death. Dad's death was horrible. Mom's death is—O.K."
Most of us who have suffered through and with our parents' dying
can empathize with Jean's mixture of feelings. The loss of a parent
after a long, slow dying is an ambivalent experience and therefore an
ambivalent grief.

Middle aged adults of the "sandwich generation" have responsibilities on both ends of life. Besides the ill or aging parent, they
also have busy work schedules, family obligations and household duties that can't wait. Amidst all of this, there is little time to grieve.
It is easy for busy adult children to ignore their own grief for their
dying or deceased parent. It is easy just to repress it or deny it or
drown it in activity. It doesn't seem as important as all the pressing
obligations of career and family.

The Ignored Grief

The loss of parents is a difficult loss for many adults because its
grief is largely ignored and under-valued in our society. The grief
that adults feel when their parent(s) die is a secret grief. It is the hidden pain that millions of adults carry around with them year after
year. Edward Myers in his book *When Parents Die* expresses this
same point of view when he writes:

> In fact, our entire culture has more or less ignored what
> adults experience following the death of their parents. Yet
> five percent of the United States population loses a parent
> within a given year. Given our current population, that
> means that 11,650,000 Americans lose a parent annually.
> Loss of a parent is the single most common form of bereave-
> ment in this country. . . . [Yet] the unstated message is
> that when a parent is middle-aged or elderly, the death is
> somehow less of a loss than other losses. The message is
> that grief for a dead parent isn't entirely appropriate.[10]

We live in an age when there is a virtual epidemic of unresolved grief
in our society. Millions upon millions of people carry the pain of a
loss with them, just below the surface of their psyches. One of the

largest, if not the largest, category of losses that remain unhealed is that of a death of a parent.

There are probably several reasons why this particular loss gets downgraded in the culture. Most people think, for example, that when a parent dies, it was expected or should have been expected. "After all, every parent will die someday." That is a normal part of life. People should expect it and therefore, by implication, should not be as upset emotionally. Second, most parents die in old age after long lives. Therefore, the assumption is that the survivors should not grieve as intensely as they might if the parent had died during their youthful years. "After all they had their life." Third, when a parent dies, especially the first parent, much of the focus of the supportive community is on the grieving spouse, not on the grieving adult child. When John's father died, he noted, "The first question out of people's mouths was, 'How is your mom doing?' The first question was rarely, if ever, 'How are *you* doing?' " The assumption is made that an adult son's or daughter's grief should not be as intense as a spouse's. That may or may not be true. Much depends on circumstances. They are different losses and most likely different griefs. In many people's minds, however, the surviving child is a grown-up, a responsible middle generation adult. He or she doesn't need our sympathy and support the way the lonely spouse does. Thus, the grief of the adult child gets ignored.

The result of this observation, if true, is that it is hard to grieve openly for our parents. We tend to bottle up the emotions faster than we might otherwise. We tend to think that we should get over it sooner and get back to work, back to our many responsibilities. There are few social supports for the mourning for our aged parents. So we don't grieve. And if our parent died an agonizing death, then we are all the more relieved than grieved. It is hard to appreciate our pain, when our mind keeps telling us how much better off they are.

Guilt in Grief

Compared to other losses and other griefs, the grief we feel for our deceased parent(s) seems unusually permeated with guilt feelings. Guilt is a normal component of grieving, but it seems especially prevalent in the mourning we experience after a parent's death.

Prior to the 1978 national conference on "You and Your Aging Parent," approximately one hundred unstructured interviews were conducted with people involved in all dimensions of the issue. Ira S. Hirschfield and Helen Dennis report: "For the adult child, the most dominant and pervasive issue regarding intergenerational relationships is the subject of guilt."[11] People feel obligated to their parents—a sense of responsibility. They want "to do right by them," especially during their last years or days of life. Guilt is a theme as one's parent ages, but it is also the dominant theme in the bereavement of the adult child. After mom or dad dies, we need some reassurance that we did all we could, that there are no untied ends, that our obligations were fulfilled. Our successful adjustment to the loss of a parent must involve the resolution of our guilt feelings.

In reference to our parents, most of us feel a generalized guilt left over from our childhood. We all have long histories, filled with pleasant and painful memories. Most of us have numerous events or issues that we feel guilty about with our parents—some things we did not perform well, some words we shouldn't have said, some obligations we forgot about. Usually these are events that have long since been forgotten by our parents—but we have not forgotten. Just below the surfaces of our adult facades, there is still a little girl or a little boy that wants daddy's recognition or mommy's embrace more than anything else in all the world. And in the mind of that little girl or little boy, we still may feel that we have never quite earned either the recognition or the embrace. This kind of generalized guilt is almost universal with parents and their adult children. It is there in our grieving.

Sometimes the guilt in our grief is related to the unexpressed anger or resentments we feel toward our parents. Physician Smiley Blanton, writing about the middle aged adult, says,

> We must always keep in mind the psychiatric truth that where our parents are concerned we have an ambivalent attitude: we love them, but we also resent them. . . . The memory of them still exists in us, below the conscious level, and the corresponding resentments exist too.[12]

We all feel some disappointment in our parents. It's an inevitable part of growing up. Some people get this disappointment worked through before their parents die. Others do not and carry their resentment into their bereavement. It is hard to be angry with the deceased when we're supposed to feel sorrowful. "I'm angry, but I can't be angry. I feel guilty that I feel angry at these 'wonderful' people to whom I should be eternally grateful." Do you hear the guilt in the anger?

Another piece of the guilt that we might feel in relation to our parents' death may have to do with particular decisions we had to make for mom or dad involving their living arrangements or medical care. If we had to place mom in a nursing home against her wishes, then that can bother us. Or if we decided to let dad live alone after mom died, instead of taking him into our home, we may feel guilty about that. Or if we were not able to be present at the moment of death, then that may bother us. Or if we were not as supportive or as thoughtful as we felt we should have been (or as much as a sibling was), then that may bother us too.[13] All of these real or perceived "sins" may bother us and become the particulars of our guilt.

In the process of losing our parents, it is almost impossible to avoid having to make difficult medical, legal and financial decisions regarding our parents' welfare. Here is where we really earn our keep as sons or daughters. There are no easy decisions, and if this is our last parent and if we are also the only child available, then the burden of these decisions falls squarely on our shoulders. In particular the medical decisions and the question of "heroic measures" lingers in the back of our minds. Most of us are laymen (or laywomen) when it comes to the high-tech world of modern medicine and hospital care. We can be easily overwhelmed and confused by conflicting medical terms, procedures and even the differing types of doctors. How far shall we go in trying to prolong a parent's life? How far would Mom or Dad want us to go? When is there no chance for a full recovery, or even a partial recovery? When do we "pull the plug"? And who makes that decision?[14]

Working with guilt feelings seems to be a process of sorting through the events, scenes and conversations that bother us most. Part of our grief work is to talk through all of the factors and situations. The troublesome events may be recent or those of many years

earlier. Sometimes we have to go over them again and again, so as
to clear our minds. We have to try to decide if we did the right thing
or the not-so-right thing. The only solution for legitimate guilt is a
full acceptance of God's forgiveness. Some of the guilt feelings associated with bereavement are not so legitimate though, and we
must wrestle more with forgiving ourselves.

Tony tortured himself for years about his mother's death. "It
was handled all wrong," he thought. "I wasn't there when she died,
as she requested. You know she asked me to do that, on the phone
about a week before she died. She said, 'Honey, when the time
comes, you be here. Will you?' I assured her that I would be there.
She had always counted on me since dad died. She was really scared
of dying alone."

Unfortunately, Tony's mother did die alone in the middle of the
night. Tony couldn't get there fast enough. Now he can't forgive himself. Intellectually he knows that he couldn't have gotten there, but
emotionally he can't let go of it. It hurts too much. The image of his
mother dying alone haunts him. "After all that mother did for me,
that was the least I could have done for her," he mourned, "but I
couldn't come through."

I remember the day that Tony began to get some relief from this
guilt. It came during a dramatic role play that he and a woman therapist were engaged in. In acting out an imaginary conversation between Tony and his mother, the therapist kept saying "I forgive you
. . . I forgive you . . . I forgive you." I must have counted forty times
that this phrase was said, and each time the words cut deeper and
deeper into Tony's soul. He had never really let those words in so
deep before. Up to now he had known about forgiveness, but had
not experienced it. Tony's tears flowed long and hard. It was a different kind of grief now, a grieving for his failure, for his lost ideal,
for his sins. It made possible the beginning of self-forgiveness.

Baggage from the Past

We have a tendency to idolize our parents just by virtue of their
being our parents. We all begin life as very dependent creatures,
called children. During those years we perceive our parents to be

like little gods. That is how it appears from the vantage point of a three year old. Mother and father appear to be all-powerful, ever-present and all-knowing. A part of the normal developmental process is a growing out of this kind of primitive dependency or parental idolatry. In time we come to see our parents as humans. Like us they are prone to mistakes; like us, they cannot be everywhere at once; and like us, they are not perfect. Yet, not everyone comes to this kind of mature perspective on his or her parents. Some people still make mom or dad into little gods, giving them unusual powers to determine their values and their self-worth. In grief, the tendency to idolize is even stronger, fueled as it is by a mistaken desire to honor their memory.

Joan's relationship with her father had always been a rocky one. As a child, the only girl, she wanted her father's attention, but could never seem to get it no matter how hard she tried. He was a critical and demanding father who gave little praise but plenty of advice. Particularly during her adolescent years she rebelled often and did some pretty foolish things, all designed in one way or another to attract his attention. Her father just ignored her even more. He seemed to be more interested in her brothers and their assorted accomplishments than in Joan's antics. Joan grew into adulthood, feeling that she was never ever going to be good enough.

Over the years, Joan's father mellowed a great deal and Joan grew up, married and had a family. Dad seemed to converse more with her as he got older. He wasn't so crusty and aloof. He seemed to take genuine delight in Joan's children, who in turn loved going to visit their grandpa. Only through her own children did Joan feel any partial approval by her father. Yet, it was an ambivalent feeling for Joan to see her father bestowing more affection on her children than she felt she ever received from him herself.

In Joan's grief, following her father's untimely death, all of these old issues surfaced. Joan's bereavement was permeated by a depression. She had a sickening sense that it was now too late, too late to earn his respect, too late to rescue her self-esteem. To make matters worse, she had failed him again. Her mom reported that the Sunday before he died, he was complaining that Joan did not bring the grandchildren by to see him. Two days later he died. Joan can see the frown on his face as clear as day. Even from his grave, he was disapproving of her. Now in her grief she longed for his love all the more. Through her tears, she would say, "If only he was still here, even for a day, perhaps he would love me. Perhaps we would have that conversation that I always wanted to have." Yet in her calm moments, she knew so well that words had always come hard between them. Despair dominated her grieving. It seemed that there was no chance for her now, no hope. All of her self-acceptance was buried with him. From her perspective she was left with nothing but her inadequacies.

Joan had great trouble with her grief work. On one hand she idolized her father more in her sorrow than she had done in real life. Daddy became all powerful in death. His approval alone mattered—but now there was no hope. She would never earn his respect now. She was condemned to live out her days without full acceptance.

Obviously Joan had tons of baggage left over from the past that contaminated her grief process. She never experienced much healing until she recognized all of this baggage and began to wrestle with the whole of her relationship with her father. For it was all tied up in her grief. In the terminology of this book, she "idolized" her father. Her operational theology read, "I will be saved only when father approves of me" and she carried this belief right into her bereavement. In fact grieving only intensified the feelings all the more. Ultimately for Joan, salvation was not to be found in worshiping the dead, but in taking back her own power and then in rooting her worth in a God whose love transcends the losses and idols of this world.

Can't Go Home Again

Another theme experienced by many in the loss of their parents is the awareness that they have lost more than these two individuals, even more than these two current parents. They have lost the parents of yesterday, the parents of their childhood and youth.

In grieving over a parent's death, there is this tendency to review all of the memories of childhood. John, for example, says that when his father died, he remembered the times they went fishing together when he was a kid. "All through the funeral," shared John,

"I kept thinking of one fishing trip after another. They were good memories, tender memories, but I hadn't thought of most of them in years." In grieving for our parents, we remember the full scope of our history with them.

Yes, we know that we lost our childhood years ago when we grew up and left home. It seemed O.K. then. We were going on to something else. But now when our parents die, we feel as if we are losing our childhood all over again. Maybe we are losing our history. Our parents are the story keepers, the keepers of the hundred and one funny stories about our childhood. They know all our past.[15] They know who we were and how we have become what we are. We lose our parents, yes, but we also lose something else—our childhood. We grieve for both.

When my own father lay dying in a hospital, each of us had time to make our peace with him. That was one of the few advantages of his prolonged battle with death. I remember my last words to him so well. Dad had drifted off into a coma a couple days earlier, so most of my last time with him was just me sitting holding his hand, talking to him here and there. The time had come for me to leave. I knew very well this might be my last time to see him alive. The words just came tumbling out, "Goodbye, daddy. I love you." I was a little bit surprised at them myself. I hadn't called him "daddy" in probably thirty years, but it seemed right. It was as though I was saying goodbye not just to the "dad" of today, but to the "daddy" of yesterday too. "Goodbye, daddy."

There is a strange intangible feeling that people have about their parents and their home. No matter how old we get, we think that we can always go home again. Was it Robert Frost who defined home as that place where if you go, they have to take you in? Middle-aged adults really don't go home much, but it's nice knowing that it is there.

"Sometimes when I am sick with a cold," says Holly, "but I can't stop to rest—kids must get to practice; the laundry is piling up—I say to myself, I'm going home to mom." "She will make me a big bowl of home-made soup," Holly fantasizes, "and I'll curl up on the couch with a good book, watch a little TV, and Mom and I will talk until 2 A.M." There is a part of us, like Holly, that thinks that we can always go home again, even if we never do. When our parents die, that fantasy is shattered. We can't go home again.

The process of working through our parents' will, estate and personal possessions evokes similar kinds of feelings. The process of dissolving the family home carries with it many of these same feelings of the loss. Have you had the experience of sitting down with your siblings and dividing up the possessions of your parents' home? It is an unpleasant task, one that many of us would just as soon avoid. It can be very sad. Each possession or memento is a part not just of their life, but of our life as well. We have memories and feelings about the our parents' possessions. It is not just their life, but our life that we are dividing up as well. [16] We have not just lost them, our beloved parents, but we have lost a part of ourselves as well—our past, our childhood, our home.

New Identity, New Life Stage

All losses have an eschatological dimension to them. All losses make us aware of the shortness of time. The death of one's parent(s) seems to accent this awareness in a special way. We, the adult children, become more aware that the older generation has passed on and that now our generation rises to the position of leadership. This awareness changes family roles and identities.

When Jim's father died, he reported, "I was aware of how I became the eldest man in the family. There was no one else to look up to. My younger sister used to call dad a lot, but now she calls me. Dad's death made a difference in my role. I wasn't sure I was ready for it. There is a part of me that doesn't want to be head of this family. I don't want the responsibility. I'm not that old." The death of a parent brings on these kinds of changes in family dynamics and interactions. It is inevitable. In a sense dying is a family affair.

When Cloyce's father died, she was approaching her mid-life crisis. He was a well-known minister in the New York area, a popular speaker, and an influential and strong personality. He died unexpectedly of a heart attack after church one day. There were hundreds at his funeral. As the eldest child of four, Cloyce participated in the funeral service, saying some things on behalf of the family. That was when it really hit her that she had to do it. She had wanted to be a minister most all of her life, but in those days women just didn't become preachers, and besides she kept waiting for one of the boys to follow in dad's footsteps. They never did, and in the meanwhile she did everything but preach in her local church. There was something about his death that crystallized her own call. Now she knew that it was now or never. The following week she enrolled in the seminary. Her only regret was that he couldn't have been there to officially "lay on the hands" in her ordination ceremony three years later. He would have been proud.

There is something about the death of one's parents that seems to make us aware of this "now or never" dimension to life. Now we are the next generation. The torch has been passed. Our role has changed. We have a new identity and a new opportunity for growth. We may pick up the torch or not, as we wish. But regardless, the torch has been passed. The death of our parents has a way of calling us to be what we are meant to be.

The world is a different place after our parents die. On the one hand the world seems more empty now, more stripped of illusions and comforts, more alone in a deep existential way. On the other hand, when our parents die, we seem to come of age. We pass on into a new stage in life's journey, a time of generativity, a time of "filial maturity," a time of fulfillment. We now take our place "center stage." We take up the artist's brushes and for better or worse leave our mark on life's canvas. This new life stage can be the most productive and creative of our life cycle. But it will be so only if we are able to say "goodbye" to our parents and not cling to them in varying degrees of idolization. The living God bids us to grieve. For only in grief will we again find new life.

Notes

1. See National Center for Health Statistics, U.S. Department of Health, Education and Welfare, *Vital Statistics of United States: 1974, Vol 2, Section 5, Life Tables* (Washington, D.C.: U.S. Government Printing Office, 1976).

2. R. Thomas Gillaspy, "The Older Population: Considerations for Family Ties," in Pauline K. Ragan, editor, *Aging Parents* (Los Angeles: University of Southern California Press, 1979), p. 14.

3. See Judith Treas, "Intergenerational Families and Social Change," in *Aging Parents*, pp. 58–65.

4. In fact as the life span continues to lengthen even further, it may become more and more common for adult children to still be caring for an aged parent even after they themselves have entered retirement. Bernice L. Neugarten, for example, now says that we have to talk about the middle generations in the plural, and conceive of a family structure of four and five generations. See her article, "The Middle Generations," in *Aging Parents*, pp. 258–266.

5. The actual research on this point is of mixed results. Some studies suggest that most older Americans live within one hour of at least one of their children. Other studies have indicated that fifty percent of older Americans have no living relative close at hand. For a summary of this material, see James A. Peterson's article, "The Relationships of Middle-Aged Children and Their Parents," in *Aging Parents*, pp. 27–36.

6. Dependency in old age is actually related more to declining mental and physical functioning than to any particular age. The so-called "young old" are still very independent and often see their children's caring as premature.

7. Dr. Missinne made this observation in the "Adventure in Aging Workshop" at Pilgrim Place, Claremont, California on August 8, 1986.

8. Occasionally we can even experience some anger/frustration that our ailing parent doesn't die sooner and "get it over with," so we can get on with our lives. This is a difficult type of anger to manage.

9. The most obvious thing that would be helpful is for family members to discuss such issues ahead of time and perhaps make use of a living will.

10. Edward Myers, *When Parents Die: A Guide for Adults* (New York: Viking Penguin, 1986), p. 5.

11. Ira S. Hirschfield and Helen Dennis, "Perspectives," in *Aging Parent*, p. 3.

12. Smiley Blanton, *Now or Never: The Promise of the Middle*

Years (Carmel, New York: Guideposts Associates, 1959), p. 236. Dr. Blanton, along with Rev. Norman Vincent Peale, founded the Institute for Religion and Health in New York City.

13. Many grieving people "act out" their guilt through the funeral and its related trappings. The funeral industry has been severely criticized over the years for playing on this inevitable guilt in the survivor's sorrow. Yet, in another sense I have witnessed occasions when an ostentatious funeral actually helped release a grieving adult child from a plaguing sense of guilt. Perhaps it was so because he or she could now do something concrete to make it up to mom or dad. Forgiveness can be secured in strange ways.

14. These are difficult decisions. Fortunately there are many fine books being written on the subject of medical ethics these days. In addition many hospitals have clinically trained chaplains or pastoral counselors who can assist you with ethical decisions.

15. Parents and grandparents are typically the keepers of the family history. Following the book and television series "Roots," there has been more interest among families in recording the family histories before parents die. In addition to its historical value, it is a valuable experience in anticipatory grieving.

16. In recent years with the "farm crisis" in this country, we have seen stories of families being forced to dissolve the family farm or homestead after generations of the same family worked it. I can imagine that the grief experienced here is powerful and includes the loss of home, loss of roots and a loss of history.

Chapter 6

The Loss of Work

" . . . and they burned incense to other gods, and worshiped the works of their own hands" (Jer 1:16).

Most all of us work throughout the adult years of our lives, both outside of the home and inside. Most of us invest ourselves in our jobs. They are activities that we take some pride in, activities that we feel reflect on us and give our lives meaning. In our adult years we tend to define ourselves by our work. Some of us even have something more than a job. We have a lifelong investment in a particular line of work or area of activity. We have a career.

So it is, then, that one of the major losses in the later years is the loss of work. Sooner or later each of us will give up, voluntarily or involuntarily, our life's work. This loss may come abruptly, such as at retirement, or it may come gradually as we reduce our duties with our increasing age. Eventually, we must give up our work and all the feelings of worthiness, identity and productivity that go with it.

The Changing Face of Retirement

"Retirement" in its present day form is really an invention of the twentieth century. During most of the history of western civilization (and certainly in other cultures today), people did not retire in the modern sense of the word. There was no set period of leisure at the end of life that one was entitled to as a reward for years of labor. Most humans continued to work every day of their lives and gave up work only as their decreasing energy led them to. As they aged and could not carry the expected work load, they moved into the roles of teacher, master craftsman or counselor to the younger workers. A person was never completely uninvolved in his or her craft, business or family farm. There was always work to be done. Only the respec-

tive work roles changed with increasing years. "Retirement," if anything, meant a much smaller period of time, usually when one was
totally disabled or unable to work. In those days nobody wanted to
be retired.

The nature of retirement did not change in isolation. Two other
social changes helped make possible the "new" retirement we now
enjoy. One of the factors was the financing of retirement. The social
security program was the first step in that direction. It was the first
large-scale source of retirement income outside of earned wages.
Even more importantly, the social security program changed people's expectations. Now retirement was seen more as a time to be
enjoyed. For that kind of retirement, however, money was needed.
More and more people began creating pension funds, annuities and
savings. Others began to demand that these benefits be built into the
contractual agreements between employees and employers.

Secondly, the advances in health care have made retirement
more enjoyable, more of a period of leisure instead of a brief period
forced on us by declining health. It is now possible to retire in good
health and spend many years enjoying life before encountering severe health limitations. The life expectancy of Americans has steadily
increased throughout this century. Without these advances in af-
fordability and in health care, retirement would not be possible as it
is currently constituted.

When should one retire? The wisdom on this subject has
changed over the years. Through the mid-part of this century, the
mandatory retirement age of sixty-five was accepted and generally
enforced. Yet, there has always been a great debate about the values
of compulsory retirement. There are many who preferred retirement to be a fixed point, where it could be anticipated and planned
for and where they could be "required" to let go of their work. Others resented having to give up work while they still had many good
years left.

The old adage that "retirement brings early death" fed into this
debate on the necessity of a fixed retirement age. There seemed to be
many stories of high strung workaholics who retired abruptly and
dropped dead within two weeks. When this adage was put under the
scrutiny of research, however, it did not hold up.[1] The data now suggests that there is no link between retirement per se and early death. In

fact, the opposite relationship may well be true: retirement prolongs life in most cases. The health of older citizens has generally improved so much in recent decades that now the "health argument" is used as a reason for extending the mandatory retirement age to seventy.

Currently, there is great flexibility in this nation on the subject of when to retire. Many professions, companies and unions are approaching the subject with an open mind. They are trying to look at the "abilities and capabilities" of the person instead of any fixed age. There are more and more early retirements. Many people take retirement at age sixty-two which is now permissible in the social security system. There are some executives who are given incentives to retire earlier than that and make room for a new management team. There are police officers and firefighters who can retire after twenty years of service and professional athletes who retire at age thirty-five when their bodies cannot keep up with the pace. At the other end of the scale, there are more people who choose to continue working long after age sixty-five. Some have careers where full-time work is allowed and encouraged until a maximum age of seventy. Others can "retire," but still continue working part-time at their career or at new jobs or at non-paid activities, interests and avocations.

These changes in the face of retirement seem to be largely welcomed and appear to be changes that are in a healthy direction.[2] There is such diversity among people in the later years that it seems wise to provide more options for people regarding retirement. The implication of all this for our discussion about loss of work is that the loss of work is no longer as much of a fixed event as it used to be. The loss of work is experienced by more and more people as a gradual process. The loss is not so abrupt. The change is not so dramatic. Thus, the grief that people experience related to the loss of work is also more diffused and subtle. It is less likely to be traumatic grief. It is more likely to be a gradual grieving.

Retirement and the Meaning of Work

What is clear from much of the research on retirement is that how one deals with retirement depends in large measure on the meaning that work has for that person prior to retirement. This observation should sound familiar. In our earlier discussion of grief dynamics, we noted that the strength of a person's sorrow depends on the meaning that he or she gave to the lost object. The issue is not just the strength of the meaning, however, but the varieties of meanings and unique functions that working performs in our lives. What is clear is that work carries several important meanings in our lives. We need to understand these meanings if we are to understand the nature of the loss of work.

The name Robert Havighurst has been associated with the study of work and retirement for three decades. His book *The Meaning of Work and Retirement* co-authored with Eugene A. Friedmann, is a classic in this field.[3] The studies therein have been repeated in many other times and places. The conclusions have largely stood the test of time, although they have been expanded some with each new study. The central conclusion of Havighurst's research is that there is a link between the meanings a person attaches to work and that person's adjustment to retirement.

After studying various occupational groups for many years, Havighurst currently suggests that there are six broad "social psychological meanings of work."[4] These meanings are those which are beyond the obvious purpose of work which is to provide income. The six "larger" meanings are:

1. Work is the basis for our sense of worth or self-respect. We feel good about ourselves when we work.

2. Work is a locus of social participation. We make friends and maintain friendships through our jobs.

3. Work is a source of prestige. We get recognition through the quality of our work.

4. Work includes new experiences, a chance to be creative and to achieve. Work is a means of self-expression.

5. Work is a chance to serve others. This is a meaning more associated with service-oriented work.

6. Work is a way of passing time. Work is a way of avoiding boredom.

These various meanings of work vary themselves according to the occupational group being studied. People from all occupational groups affirm that work is a source of friends, a way of passing time and a means of gaining self-respect. Some occupational groups emphasize the "service to others" meaning more than others and the "new experience" meaning is a meaning that is found only among people in the arts or similar creative professions. All occupations, however, do carry some if not all of these "extra-economic meanings." Work is more than a source of income. Work means much more. Therefore the loss of work potentially means much more too.

Overall Havighurst and other researchers[5] over the years have demonstrated a strong link between retirement adjustment and the meaning of work. They found that the people who saw work only as a way to earn money and had few "extra economic meanings" attached to their work actually preferred to retire and did so easily compared to people who had many extra-economic meanings to work. In other words if our work is just a job, nothing more, then we can let go of it easily. But if our work is also our source of self-worth, our main source of social contacts and our primary identity, then work is more difficult for us to let go of. Work means more to us, quantitatively and qualitatively. It becomes a complex loss, embedded with many sub-losses.

This understanding of the role of meaning in loss adjustment fits with our understanding of grief and bereavement. We have learned that if the lost object or lost person means more to us, then we will experience it as a greater loss and will grieve accordingly. If we assigned few meanings to that which is lost, then we will grieve lightly and easily, because our essential meanings are rooted elsewhere. The issue becomes then: How central is work to our lives? How many extra meanings do we attach to our work? Does our job carry this "extra" baggage for us? If so, then when we lose work, in part or totally, we are losing more than a mere job. We are losing self-esteem, self-definition, a source of friends and so on. From this perspective, we can readily see that the loss of work can be a significant loss in the life cycle, a loss that involves several powerful sub-losses.

Another way of talking about meanings is to talk about human needs. Meanings reflect needs. The meanings that work provides fulfill important and necessary needs. Every human being needs to have friends, needs to have a sense of self-respect, needs a clear and stable identity and so on. The problem of adjusting to retirement might then be understood as how to get these needs fulfilled in other ways, ways not associated with work. The needs are legitimate, and if they are not fulfilled in some way, a person's mental health will suffer in retirement. "The problem of retirement," writes Havighurst in the 1954 study, "is to secure the extra-economic values that work brings and to secure them through play or leisure-time activity. . . . "[6] In other words if we are to adjust well to retirement, we must learn how to get self-respect out of a leisure activity rather than out of a work activity, or how to make and keep friends through leisure activities rather than exclusively through the workplace. Havighurst has argued that leisure is capable of fulfilling all of these needs if we correctly understand the nature of leisure and learn the "arts of leisure." Furthermore, he suggests that our society will continue to become more leisure oriented, as the length of life extends further and as we become more affluent as a nation. Therefore, for Havighurst and others, the problem of retirement is the problem of leisure.[7]

The Loss of Status

One of the recurrent themes with retired persons is the loss of status or power that they feel is associated with their loss of work. Admittedly, this theme is more reflective of persons who had some sense of status or power in their jobs. Executives, professionals and owners of businesses seem to feel this loss most keenly. Employees with little job status or authority tend to feel this loss less keenly.

Vern was a merchant all of his life. He learned the trade from his European father, although not the specific business. Vern started a small grocery store when he was a young man and grew up with it and through it. The store, "Vern's Market," was on the corner of Main and Elm, a landmark in this midwestern town. The store provided him with a good but modest income over the years. His four children were raised in the store, helping out on Saturdays, stocking shelves, sweeping floors. Sometimes he paid them a little something. Sometimes it was just expected. Over the years Vern's store grew with the town. He expanded several times, buying two adjacent buildings, adding hardware lines, home products and various services. In his later years the store was more than he could handle. He gradually gave it over to his youngest son, who was the only child of the four who showed much interest in the place. Vern couldn't do the work anymore, but he still liked to call the shots from the back room.

Retirement was never discussed in Vern's family as such. It happened gradually. Vern could not do the heavy work anymore, and he had to give up the early morning trips to the produce mart. Johnny began to do those tasks. As Vern faded out more, Johnny assumed a greater and greater role in the daily management of the store. It was hard for Vern to see Johnny running things, especially when he ran things differently than Vern had. In addition Johnny had some new ideas that he wanted to try out, but was reluctant to go against father's wishes. Johnny didn't feel free to implement his ideas, because Papa was still "in charge"—sort of. Vern couldn't stay out of the store, but neither could he keep up with the demands. The conflicts increased, and at one point Johnny threatened to quit: "Either you let me run the store or you run it yourself, Dad. You can't have it both ways. It's time for you to let go of it." That seemed to help Vern see things a little more clearly. Johnny was right. Vern didn't want the hard work of the store, but he did like having the reins of power. It was the power that was the hardest thing to let go of.

About this time I asked Vern what he missed most about work. He said it was "not the work . . . too hard now, too difficult!

"You have to get up so early in the morning, and the 'fussy customers.' No, I don't miss that. . . .

"I miss being the boss though. I like making my own decisions. I like the fact that everyone in town knows me. . . .

"It was hard for me to let Johnny take over. He's a good boy, but I was so afraid he was going to ruin everything I have built up. It was real hard to watch him do it his way. . . . "

Vern did have a hard time giving up the power associated with his work, as modest a power as it was. About a year after this interview, however, he and his wife went on a six-month tour of the nation in a motor home. It was something that he always wanted to do, but in retailing "you don't get many vacations." It was a delightful experience—the vacation that he never had. It also helped to separate him emotionally from his work. When he got back, Johnny was finally and really "in charge."

How people adjust to retirement depends on what they are losing. If their job had status, then they lose status. Yet responsibility can be a burden as well as a privilege, as any merchant like Vern could tell us. Some retirees, when they really stop and think about it, are just as glad to get out from under the burden of power. Usually what they miss most is the trappings of power. They miss the status, the money, the prestige, the ability to order people around and get what you want when you want it.

Unfortunately there are few rituals that formalize and facilitate retirement or the transfer of power. Retirement parties come closest. Installation ceremonies also try to facilitate transfers of power. Facilitating the loss of work can sometimes be helped by finding ways to help retirees maintain a sense of status even in retirement. Titles, such Professor Emeritus, help those who have retired to see themselves as still valuable. A good ritual would both comfort the participants and facilitate their grieving. For many people a major part of the loss of work issue is the accompanying loss of power and status.

Loss of Friends

Most people find that their work is a source of friendship. Its degree of importance will vary from person to person. Some people make lifelong friends in and through their work. Others form work-only friendships. Either way, work friendships can be an important piece in our social network and support system.

There is something very profound about the nature of work being communal. Work forces humans to cooperate. Several anthropologists, notably Richard Leaky, are saying that the key to the success of human evolution is cooperation, not competition.[8] It wasn't that humans were more competitive than other species or more aggressive, but that humans were more cooperative than other species. Cooperation has led to our dominance as a species. Work requires that humans cooperate. Work throws people together in a common task, sometimes in common suffering, and thereby creates friendship. Often what we miss most in the loss of work is the daily contact with friends, the esprit de corps and the genuine joy at a job well done.

Vivian is a seventy-one year old retired school teacher. She began her career as a teacher in mid-life, after her husband died an early death in an auto accident. She needed a job in those days to finish raising her two girls. She worked as an elementary school teacher, mostly in the same school for over twenty-five years. She retired late, at age seventy, according to the new flexible retirement rules adopted by the school district. The last few years of her career, she was made a "Master Teacher" and spent a portion of her day "coaching" the younger teachers (actually they were all younger than she) in the arts of teaching. In retirement she lived alone, not too far from the school where she worked so long.

"The thing I miss most about my work," she remarked once, "is the children. I miss the children. I loved having children around me. I loved helping them, seeing them master a concept or paint a picture or sound out words for the first time. They were like a big family to me, and every year I got a new bunch. Some of them still keep in touch with me, you know. . . . I cannot take it like I used to, though. They wear me out more now. I miss the children, but I am also glad not to have them around all the time."

"I miss the school and my fellow teachers," she continued. "Teaching really became my social life during those years after Willard died. I socialized with my fellow teachers. Some of them became my best friends; in fact, they still see me occasionally and send me cards on my birthday and all . . . It was hard adjusting to living without friends at first. I do not think that I have done it very well. I get lonely still and sometimes I just go for a walk, down past the school."

If we have used our work as the main source of our friendships over the years, then we are in for a difficult transition to retirement. We may want to find some way to stay involved marginally with our career, even if just for the social contacts. Other retirees may need to find new sources of friendship. There are many sources of friendship beside work—service clubs, neighborhoods, churches, interest groups and so on. There are many places and sources of friendship, but they all must be pursued.

What many people discover in retirement is that their work was a built-in source of friends. Friendship was automatic, and so they didn't have to work at it. After they retire, however, the friendship isn't so automatic. They have to be more intentional about friendship. They have to work at it. It won't happen otherwise. They have to make it happen. That involves work. This shift in one's expectations about friends and friendships is subtle but very important. Some retirees do not make this shift and just sit at home wondering why they are lonely.

The nice thing about being intentional about friendship is that we can choose not to socialize too. When we worked for a living, we were thrown together with people whether we wished to be or not. There were probably a few people that we did not want to socialize with, but were expected to. To some extent we had to socialize in the workplace. In retirement, however, there is the freedom not to socialize and to be more selective about one's friends. Friendship is now intentional, now something we have to choose. That's the beauty of it and its difficulty.

The loss of friendship is one of the dimensions of the loss of work that can be difficult for many people. It involves a restructuring of where and how one socializes. It involves learning to "work at" making friends more than perhaps one had to in the past. Yet, making and maintaining friendships in old age is very important. It is one of the factors that is positively correlated with good mental and physical health. So, adjusting well to the loss of work must include a learning to be intentional about friendship.

Retirement and the Idolization of Work

When we lose work, either totally or partially, we go through an adjustment process that can be very grief-like. There are so many variables that influence the character of this process that it is hard to describe a uniform process for everyone. Much depends on the meanings that we have attached to our work and on how much preparation, emotionally and financially, we have done for retirement. Nevertheless, it is not uncommon to have feelings of loss, confusion and meaninglessness during the first few months after retirement. In such situations, it is important to try to identify what exactly we are grieving. Are we grieving the loss of work? the loss of status? the loss of friends? or the loss of income? We can be grieving any and all of these things.

In time most people adjust to retirement. They learn to find new activities. They learn to find new sources of friends and new meanings. They learn to live with reduced income. But what if they do not adjust? What about the person who can't seem to let go of work and all that it has meant to him or her.

Terry was a police officer his whole working career. He had wanted nothing else when he was a kid. After high school he went directly to a two year college and then applied for admission to the police academy. As an officer he worked hard. He enjoyed his work. It was everything that he ever wanted a job to be. He made wonderful friendships with his fellow officers. "There is nothing like being under fire together to bring people close," he would say. Terry played on the police softball team after hours. He worked out with weights during break times. He enjoyed the whole thing—the image, the socializing, the work.

Terry was forty-two years old when he was in a car crash while chasing another vehicle. He was seriously injured and was hospitalized for several months. His injury was around the spinal cord and resulted in only partial use of his legs when he was released from the hospital. This was a major trauma for Terry and his wife, but the police force was supportive and Terry's faith was strong. He was convinced that he could repair the damage with physical therapy and weight training. He'd be back on the active duty roster in no time. Well, Terry did work hard, but progress did not come after a year nor even after two years. Finally, he was forced to apply for disability retirement. Terry's police career was over.

Retirement was not welcomed. Terry had largely denied this possibility during his recovery. He was so convinced that he could recover. Once he was declared "disabled," it seemed to snap his will to fight. He stopped trying. He gave up. He spent most of the first several months just sitting watching television. Terry did receive some disability income, but it was much less than his full salary. This added insult to injury. Now Terry's wife had to take a job. Given Terry's state of mind, she was not entirely confident in his ability to handle the children. So she arranged her work to be finished by about the time that the children came from school. Terry had gone into a deep depression. Yet, he didn't want any help, even from the department's psychiatrist. It was hard for Terry to identify his feelings, much less talk them through. It was just not part of the image.

After a while, Terry got to visiting the police station in the mornings. He would just "hang around" the coffee pot for several hours. He would time his visits so that he could have coffee with the morning shift. Most of his former colleagues did not mind Terry hanging around the station. He could be useful at times. So this pattern continued for almost another year. Terry enjoyed the station time. It helped him feel as though he was still a police officer.

In time, however, a new commander at the station came on board, and he was a person who liked to run things by the book. He confronted Terry one day, ordering him not to come by the station anymore. "Listen, Terry, this is against regulations—you hanging around here. Listen, you are not an officer. Face it. You've got to get that through your head. It's time you go."

Terry did not take those words well at all. He was angry. He stormed out of the station. He brooded about it for months, threatening "to sue the s.o.b." Yet the confrontation did force things into the open and resulted in Terry's getting professional help.

Terry's dynamics were a classic case of idolatry. Terry's job was everything to him. It was more than a means of earning a living. It was also his identity. He loved the uniform, the muscles, the force, the macho image—all of it! Police work was his life. Nothing else mattered as much. Without it, as he was now, he felt useless, like "a nobody." "If only this accident hadn't happened," he would say, "if only the doctors had fixed me up better, if only the stupid police regulations allowed me to work some, then I would be happy." Happiness could be found in going backward, not forward, thought Terry.

Terry got some help for himself and his idolatry. The secret of Terry's recovery was not at all mysterious. Basically, Terry needed to grieve. He needed to identify and express his painful feelings of loss, including sorrow, anger, guilt and depression. He needed to refashion his belief system in order to find meaning for himself in something apart from work. For Terry a piece of his recovery was found in returning to an active faith in his church. He needed to root himself "in something beyond this world," he said once. "Everything here is too temporary."

You will be interested to know that Terry eventually got work as a security guard, which was enough like police work to satisfy some of his needs, and many years after that he set up his own security business, using retired police officers (of all people). Terry's transition from work to "retirement" was long and painful. It could have been much easier and quicker if he had been able to accept reality better, or if he could have identified his grief feelings better, or if he didn't hold in his feelings as much as he did, or even if he had gotten professional help sooner. Any and all of these differences could have shortened his process.

Admittedly, few of us lose work in as early and as traumatic a way as Terry. Yet, Terry is a good example in the extreme of how a person can idolize work, a tendency that is compounded by the dynamics of bereavement. Making an idol out of work is easy to do in this society. The whole society is work oriented and tends to define and measure people by their work.[9] Finding sources of worth and identity apart from work is difficult. Terry's case is extreme in one sense, and yet in another sense there is a Terry in all of us. The tendency to make our work into an idol is a temptation that we all can fall prey to. It is something we all must deal with in making the transition to retirement, in adjusting to the loss of work.

Theology of Work and Play

This brief chapter in this small book is no place to begin a discussion of the theology of work. However, it seems to me that the nature of work is badly misunderstood in this society, and that as such it causes people a great deal of hardship at the time of retirement. It would be timely for the church to offer a vision of "good work," of how work was meant to be. Let me offer some suggestive comments along these lines.[10]

In traditional Christian thinking work is understood as either a punishment for sin or a way to avoid sinning. The Genesis story tells us that when humankind sinned and fell out of grace, one of the consequences was having to work by "sweat of your face" (Gen 3:19). In this image of work, work is negative, laborious, necessary. In contrast early Protestant theology understood work as something good, but its goodness was in its activity. Work is good because humans are supposed to be busy. Idleness is the breeding ground for sin. Therefore it is important to keep busy. It did not matter so much at what—just keep busy. These two ideas—work as a curse and work as an antidote for sin—have molded our cultural attitude toward work.[11] In both cases work is something people have to do, not something they want to do. Certainly, for most people in most places, this is how work is experienced. Yet work can be and was meant to be something more.

A theology of "good work" begins with a theology of creation. God is the Creator of the earth. God also created us in the divine image. One of the aspects of having God's image within us is that we too have the capacity to create. We, unlike other animals, can be creative. Creation has traditionally been defined as "out of nothing," in contrast to "making" which is a creating out of existing materials. Like God, humans can genuinely "create," not just "make." Our ability to create is reflected in our love for beauty, our art, our music and our desire to order and fashion the earth. In spite of the fall of humanity from innocence and our bondage to sin, our capacity to create remains.

So then what is work? Work is meant to be a way of creating. It is one way we humans have of co-creating with God. Work is self-expression. Work, at its best, is a form of love. Through work we express our God-given urge to create. All types of work can be self-expressive—design work, service work, manual work, intellectual work, industrial work. The type of work is not a limitation to its self-expressive character. When our work is "good work," it has this self-expressive character to it. It says who we are. Occasionally, we have all experienced work like this. There have been moments in our work histories when we have created something new, done something special, achieved something wonderful, and we have known the deep satisfaction that comes with this kind of work. Unfortunately in most industrial work settings, work is seldom experienced this way. For most people most of the time, work is experienced as having little intrinsic value. We therefore attach money to work in order to make it extrinsically valuable. In addition we have attached status, friendship and prestige to work for the same reason.

If we understand work as self-expression, then we can justifiably argue that humans need to work, not to avoid idleness and not because we are extrinsically motivated, but as a way of being truly what we are, as a way of co-creating with God. If we see work as self-expression, then it really does not matter whether we get paid or not. A paycheck is irrelevant to the true essence of work. The defining criteria of work is self-expression, not earning power. "Good work" can be any activity that is self-expressive. "Good work" is larger than just paid work. "Good work" includes all of the activities that we do throughout our lives that are self expressive. It includes housework, the so-called "dirty work."[12] It includes child care or elder care. It includes volunteer work. "Good work," God's created intention for human work, is valuable not for what it produces nor for what it earns us, but for the process of self-expression it affords us. If we understood work this way, there would be no degradation of persons in retirement. In fact there probably would be no retirement.

The Christian doctrine of vocation hints at this same view of "good work." It suggests that God gives each of us gifts and then calls us to fulfill those gifts in certain jobs. Each of us experiences "a calling," not just the ordained ministers. God calls each of us to fulfill our unique selves in a particular line of work, work that will allow us to express ourselves, to co-create. The distinction between an occupation and a career captures some of this sense of vocation or calling. An occupation is a job in which one "occupies" time and space. A career is an expression of our unique talents and reflects a sense of being "called" to or destined for such work. A career usually has more of this sense of work as self-expression. Each of us finds our own calling, our "good work," only in relationship to the Creator.

If we understand work as a form of self-expression, then work and play are different versions of the same creative impulse. Work and play are not opposites, not enemies. Play is also a form of self-expression. Watch children at play for awhile. What do they do? They create. They express themselves in fantasy, in art, in drama, in building. They also work in the sense that play is rehearsal for life. Someone once said that he would love to find a job that he could play at or a play that he could get paid for. Rare is the person who can work with the same joy, freedom and self-fulfillment found in play.

But isn't that what we strive for in the notion of "good work"? Isn't that what God wants for us? Work and play, properly understood, are different dimensions of the same divine image within us.

In our life cycle work and play are chronologically separated. We play as children. Then when we become adults, we work. Then when we retire, we are allowed to play again (but only if we worked hard to save enough money). The life cycle sequence is Play-Work-Play. Richard Bolles has suggested that we need to break out of these "three boxes of life."[13] We need to find ways to blend work and play together throughout our lives, and not segregate them. By segregating them, we make the transitions of life more difficult. By limiting play to childhood and retirement, we allow people to be too intense about work, too tied up in the many meanings of their work, thereby setting the stage for a difficult experience when they lose work. The loss of work would not be so difficult if we learned to play during our adult years. Similarly the loss of work would not be so difficult if we had a broader vision of work that understood "retirement" as a prime time for the realization of self-expressive work.[14]

New Challenge: A Ritual for Retirement

The church seems to be ambivalent about work. On one hand it values work. After all it keeps people from sinning and makes them responsible citizens. Yet, on the other hand, the church is appropriately suspicious of the culture's idolization of work, which has made materialists of us all. Perhaps this is why the church has not addressed the problem of developing an appropriate ritual for the life cycle transition called retirement. In my opinion there is a critical need for such a ritual.

A retirement ritual, especially a religious ritual, is a very attractive idea, one that could be an effective tool for helping people deal with both their grief feelings and their "meanings" associated with work and the loss of work. It would be a wonderful opportunity for the church to assert what it has always believed—that a person's worth can not be earned, as through his or her work, but must be accepted as a free gift of God's grace. Evelyn and James Whitehead, in writing about retirement as a religious ritual, say:

> Worth is, finally, not in productivity. Personal value is founded in something more basic than power or responsibility or salary. It rests on the rock of God's love. The cultural phenomenon of retirement can thus serve a religious function. Separating us from accumulated credentials and accustomed "proofs of merit," it invites us to acknowledge a value in life beyond and prior to human achievement.[15]

The occasion of retirement is a timely opportunity to acknowledge again that our worth, as children of God, does not depend on whether we are productive or not. Such a rite might, as the Whiteheads suggest, announce "the good news of our uselessness." What a crucial opportunity for the church to be prophetic in a society that has increasingly defined us and measured our worth by our work. On a personal level as well, such a rite could be very liberating to all who are involved in it, freeing the retiring person from old enslaving meanings, freeing him or her to enter a new stage of spiritual growth.

Several people who have also advocated a religious retirement ritual have suggested that it have a forward-looking dimension, not just a backward-looking dimension. As Thomas B. Robbs said, we need "to focus on retirement *to* instead of *from*."[16] A religious retirement ritual should include this "commissioning" element. Such a ritual would commission people, not retire them. It would empower them, not encourage their passivity. It would want to lure them forward into a new stage of life, a stage characterized by ministry, by service to others, and most importantly by a new vision of work. Toward this end, a retirement ritual would want to paint a new image of work, work as self-expression, as service to the Lord, as joyful play. It would dematerialize work and dequantify it.

The loss of work, whether it comes at retirement or at some other point in our lives, can be a growth opportunity, a chance to spiritually move beyond our limited vision of work and to see ourselves and our worth in the larger perspective of God's love. All of this is possible, however, only if we can "let go" of our old work, our old view of work and our old self-definitions and measurements of our value. We must grieve it all if we wish to move on into a still greater stage of spiritual maturity in this journey called life.

Notes

1. For a summary of this research, see Carl Eisdorfer, "Adaption to Loss of Work," in F. Carp, editor, *Retirement* (New York: Human Science Press, 1972).

2. It is an interesting contradiction that while the mandatory retirement age has gone up to age seventy, the average retirement age has actually dropped to its current 58.6 years.

3. Eugene A. Friedmann, Robert J. Havighurst, *The Meaning of Work and Retirement* (Chicago: University of Chicago Press, 1954).

4. See Robert J. Havighurst, "Life-Style and Leisure Patterns," in Richard A. Kalish, editor, *The Later Years* (Monterey: Brooks/Cole, 1977), pp. 147–156.

5. For example, see I.H. Simpson, K.W. Black and J.C. McKinney, "Work and Retirement," in I.H. Simpson and J.C. McKinney, editors, *Social Aspects of Aging* (Durham: Duke University Press, 1966), pp. 45–54.

6. Havighurst, *Meaning of Work and Retirement*, p. 189.

7. This is a point of view that I do not entirely agree with, and I will say more about it later.

8. See Richard E. Leakey, *Origins* (New York: E.P. Dutton, 1977), pp. 207–38.

9. In fact, Robert N. Bellah's recent book *Habits of the Heart: Individualism and Commitment in American Life* (Berkeley: University of California Press, 1985) suggests that themes of competition, individualism and privatization of life are becoming more (not less) pronounced in American culture as we approach the twenty-first century.

10. My comments have been informed by Dorothee Soelle's *To Work and To Love* (Philadelphia: Fortress Press, 1984) which is a provocative discussion of this topic and other related issues.

11. Admittedly, this is an over-simplification of these two important theological concepts about work. However it is often these simplified versions that shape culture so decisively.

12. The degradation of housework and homemaking may be linked to the sexism of our culture. Men have defined work that does not include a paycheck as of little value, and unfortunately many

women, who otherwise would have preferred being at home, have bought that perception.

13. See Richard N. Bolles, *The Three Boxes of Life* (Berkeley: Ten Speed Press, 1981).

14. The problem of retirement is not, as some scholars suggest, a problem of leisure, how to learn to be better consumers and content with leisure activities. Each stage of life should include a blending of work and play. Therefore retirement should not be thought of as the absence of work, but as the time for what Paul Tournier calls a "Second Career," for a type of work that is both work/play, two forms of creative self expression.

15. Evelyn Eaton Whitehead and James D. Whitehead, "Retirement," in William M. Clements, editor, *Ministry with the Aging: Design, Challenges, Foundations* (New York: Harper and Row, 1981), p. 133.

16. Thomas Bradley Robb, *The Bonus Years: Foundations for Ministry with Older Persons*, p. 96.

Chapter 7

The Loss of Spouse

"The Lord is near to the brokenhearted, and saves the crushed in spirit" (Ps 34:18).

Marriage is the most intimate of life's many relationships. The bond between husband and wife can be deep, tender and long-lasting. Thus the loss of our spouse can be one of life's most devastating emotional experiences. One half of us will have this experience, whether we wish it or not. It is the price of love. Most of us do not anticipate this loss very well, even though it is so inevitable. We had hoped to "grow old together." Yet, relatively few marriages last into the sixth, seventh and eighth decades of life. Most of us must cope with the last years of life alone. The loss of spouse is one of the most significant losses of the later years, and how we cope with this loss colors our physical, mental and spiritual health for the remainder of our lives.

The Multifaceted Loss

Unlike any other loss, the loss of our spouse is a multifaceted loss, a loss that can be devastating precisely because it is so comprehensive in scope. When we have been married for as long as forty or fifty years, we have spent more time being married than not. Our bond to our life partner is strong and complex. We have grown together, suffered together, worked together and loved together. Hopefully, we have become best friends. Losing a spouse after these many years and after this kind of relationship is the most painful kind of loss. The adjustment required by this kind of loss is massive. It affects every area of one's life.

Marian was married early in life. She and Michael were high school sweethearts from a small rural town upstate. She barely finished high school herself when her first child arrived. Michael started working as a plumber's helper, and over the years he advanced to become a journeyman plumber. They never had much in the way of material things, but they worked hard and raised four children altogether. By contemporary standards Marian was a timid person, but a loyal and dependable mother and wife. She never worked outside of the home. When Michael died at the relatively young age of forty-seven, the children were mostly adults. The transition from mother, homemaker and wife to widow, wage earner and single person was tough for Marian.

Within the span of what seemed like a few years, Marian was forced to make several significant changes, in fact more changes than she had made at any other period in her life. She began managing her own (now limited) money for the first time. She learned to live alone. She began working outside of the home. She had to assert herself more and not rely on others to protect her. She had to learn to socialize outside of her immediate family. All of these social, psychological and vocational changes were forced upon Marian by the advent of one loss.

Some years later, after Marian had made many of these changes, she reflected, "I really wasn't prepared for the single life. In fact, I got married early as a young girl partly to avoid being single. It was secure going from my father's house to Michael's house. But when Michael died, I was forced to grow up in ways that I never did earlier. And . . . " with a touch of sadness, "and I now have the whole rest of my life to learn it."

One of the questions that Marian's story raises is what it is exactly that is lost in the death of a spouse. The loss of a spouse is actually composed of several losses. Certainly, we have lost the person, the unique individual that we have known and loved for many years. Moreover, we have also lost all of the roles or functions that this person fulfilled in our lives. Our spouse was a lover and sexual partner. He or she was a provider. He or she was our companion. He or she was a household manager, accountant and a repair person. Our spouse was also a co-parent to our children. When we lose our spouse we may lose any or all of these roles as well. Each one of these losses will by itself require adjustment and change for the survivor.

In addition, the loss of our spouse will bring with it what are called "secondary losses." Some typical secondary losses include: loss of income, loss of home, loss of work or of a life style without working. Hopefully a widowed person has some financial cushion that can mitigate some of the harshness of these secondary losses. Not every widow, however, has this kind of cushion, and some must move within months or take a job within weeks of their spouse's death. In such cases the secondary loss may actually become more difficult to adjust to than the primary loss of a mate. When we speak of secondary losses, we also must be concerned about the cumulative effect of such losses. When losses pile upon losses, then we can become overwhelmed and potentially crippled. This is the danger that resides in the loss of spouse. The death of our spouse is unique among all of the losses in the later years, precisely because of its multifaceted character. Its scope is comprehensive.

Feminization of Death

The loss of a spouse is largely a women's issue in our culture. Some writers have suggested that widowhood is to women what retirement is to men.[1] That adage could be argued with, but the facts cannot be argued with. The vast majority of older Americans are women. In fact seventy percent of all women over the age of seventy-five are widowed.[2] Anyone who has ever observed a random group of elderly people will notice this obvious and painful truth. Most of the time the man dies first, leaving the widowed wife to carry on without him. Women typically outlive their male partners. Men tend to die earlier in life for a variety of psychological and physiological reasons. The result is that there are many more elderly women than men.

Few women, particularly women who have been raised in more traditional ways, are prepared to live independent lives. Women are molded in this culture to be more socially and emotionally dependent. Yet it is the woman who is more often than not left alone after the death of a spouse. It is the woman who must learn to live independently. Few men need to make this adjustment because either they die young or they remarry more frequently and more quickly than women do. Lynn Caine, whose personal story of widowhood is told in the book *Widow*, sums up her advice to women:

What is the "moral" of all this? I'm afraid the lesson is that women must learn to be more self-sufficient, more whole. Women must prepare themselves to be able to live alone. Because the majority of women will have to, eventually.[3]

I would think that given the inevitability of spousal death and the feminization of this loss, we as a culture could do more to prepare women for this loss and its transition.[4] Most women, in my experience, are inadequately prepared.

Now add on top of this concern the research that has demonstrated a link between a person's physical health and bereavement. Colin Murray Parkes, among others, has clearly demonstrated through his study of London widows that during the first year of conjugal bereavement, widows are at a high risk for all kinds of illnesses, mental and physical, including such catastrophic illnesses as cancer and heart disease.[5] Grief, particularly intense grief, is stressful to the body as well as to the mind. Little wonder that the mortality rate for all bereaved people is higher than for non-bereaved persons of the same age and status.

With all of these concerns, mental, social and physical, women need to be more thoroughly prepared for the transition from marriage to widowhood than they are. Preparation could begin with just an honest realization that for most women this loss is inevitable. It has been my experience, however, that of all of life's losses this is the one that people are least prepared for mentally, socially and financially. Even though we know it will happen, there is something about the prevailing myths about love, romance and marriage that lead most people to avoid any serious mental or emotional preparation for this loss. So it is then that more people than not, especially women, seem to be ill prepared for the loss of their spouse.

The Unexpected Loss

The loss of our spouse can come in many ways and forms. Probably the most difficult is through a sudden death. This is often the circumstance surrounding the death of the first spouse and it is therefore more likely to be the woman's experience of the death of her husband. The unexpected death catches us by surprise. It shatters our denial systems and illusions that "love will last forever." The unexpected loss causes us some unique emotional difficulties.[6]

Shock and disbelief are the two dominant themes in the early responses to sudden loss. The psychological shock we experience is not unlike the physical shock that our bodies go through when faced with a similar sudden physical trauma. The function is the same. The purpose of shock is to shut down the psyche, "to pull the circuit breaker" and to turn off the power. We are overloaded. We cannot cope with that much pain, with that much trauma all at once. So our psyches shut down. Time out!

Most people experience a numbing effect right after they hear the news of an unexpected death. In Lifton's classic study of the survivors of the atomic blast at Hiroshima, he described shock as "psychic numbing" and said that people just "ceased to feel."[7] We don't experience too many actual atomic explosions, but emotionally many sudden deaths feel as traumatic as a bomb blast. We can be just as shocked. When we are in shock, we tune out emotionally. We walk about in a daze, preoccupied or in what one person called "a mild trance." People talk and we mumble something back. We forget what. We say, "I can't believe this is happening." "No, not me! Not now! Not my Jim or my Alice!" That is disbelief and shock.

Mel's wife died suddenly in a car accident. She was in her early sixties as was her husband. Mel experienced all of the classic shock symptoms. He noted some months later, "You know, pastor, the thing that really helped me the most to come to terms with Marge's death was the viewing. Not too many people came to the viewing. I guess people don't like those things these days—but it sure helped me. There is nothing like the cold, dead body of your wife to help you really realize that she is dead. I must have sat there for hours, most of the time alone. It took that long—but gradually it sunk in: 'She's dead, Mel. She is dead!' " Rituals can be tools, as in Mel's case, to help widowed spouses break through the shock and disbelief. They also can help reinforce denial. Much depends on how the ritual is structured and conducted.

Shock can last for few hours or several days. Gradually it gives way to panic, emotional release and anger. Disbelief now alternates more frequently with periods of weeping, mourning and emotional release. Soon we have entered into the full throes of our grief work. When death comes unexpectedly, grief is usually very intense, very volatile. There was little time to prepare ourselves emotionally. There was no time for anticipatory grief. Like it or not, we are thrust into a process we cannot control or avoid. The only way out is through.

Often when a spouse dies unexpectedly, the last time we were together becomes very important. We remember vividly the last scene, the last words, the last embrace. Every detail is vivid in our memory. The colors, sounds, place, the touch of his or her hand, the subtle meanings that only we know. It is as though somebody pressed the "freeze" button on the videocassette player and the movie of our life froze at this last scene.

If our last memory of our beloved spouse was pleasant, then we are indeed fortunate. We have a nice memory to comfort us in our sorrow. Many other people are not so fortunate. Perhaps they were not able to be present when the spouse died and they wanted to be. Perhaps in that last conversation there was something more they wanted to say, but didn't. Or perhaps the last conversation was an argument or a negative exchange. They left feeling unfinished, saying to themselves, "I'll straighten this out tomorrow," but unfortunately tomorrow never comes. Or perhaps they made a promise that they couldn't fulfill. All of these things can now be haunting our souls.

If the frozen "last scene" of our beloved spouse is negative, then in our sorrow we must work to soften these mental images. If we are to grieve well, we must do some intentional editing of our mental movie. Erase those negatives scenes, if they are such. Choose to go back to an earlier time, prior to the last contact, and focus on another scene that you feel is more representative of how you feel about your deceased spouse or one that is more representative of your relationship as a whole. Focus on that scene. Dwell on it. Allow it to comfort you and speak to you in your sorrow.

What strikes people so forcibly in the case of the sudden or unexpected loss is the finality of it all. He or she is gone now. Our beloved sweetheart whom we have known most of our lives is gone, is suddenly nowhere to be found. "There isn't anywhere on the entire face of the earth where I can go and find him/her." We can't call our spouse anymore on the phone. We can't pretend that he or she is just out of town for a while. He or she is gone now, and somehow, some way, we must find the strength to go on.

Loss by Divorce

The loss of one's spouse can come not only by death, but also by divorce. Divorce is nothing new. In the last fifty years or so, we have seen a significant increase in the number of divorces in our society. Many of these divorces come early in the life of the marriage and are followed by a second marriage. Yet, for the woman who divorces late in life, say over the age of fifty, the probability of remarriage is small. This is less the case with men. Given the realities of the sex ratios of the population and the preferred age differentials between men and women, a woman who is divorced after age fifty has relatively little opportunity to remarry.[8] For all intents and purposes divorce is "as good as a death." She will probably live the rest of her life alone. That is harsh news for most women. The fantasy of remarriage dies hard.

Beverly was fifty-four years old when her marriage dissolved. It had been "dead" for many years prior to that. There was little communication, no sexual intimacy and no cooperation on even basic household decisions. Max had long ago set up a separate bank account for himself, leaving Beverly with the joint account. Beverly had taken a part-time job as a payroll clerk some years earlier which later after the divorce evolved into a full-time position. "I suppose that we just stayed together out of convenience," said Bev. "It was easier than anything else." In the last few years of the marriage, however, Max began to be abusive, not just verbally as he had always been, but physically abusive. In addition he had taken up with a younger girlfriend and went out of his way to flaunt it in Beverly's face. All of this finally pushed Beverly to file for the divorce. "Convenience" was no longer worth it.

Whether she knew it or not at the time, Beverly had entered the next stage of her life. Initially she had fantasies about remarriage "someday," but objectively the prospects were not good. She had gained considerable weight in later years and was by her own admission very "plain" looking. She was more of the "den mother type." She was hardly the type for the single bars, and as a lifelong Catholic, she soon came to realize that "one marriage was enough for her."

Beverly's experience of the loss of her spouse was considerably different from the person who loses a beloved spouse through death. For Beverly there was little grief and sorrow. Her "mourning" was colored more by anger, despair and helplessness. She had years of resentful feelings toward Max, most of which were internalized into self-blame and depression (and weight gain). Yet for Beverly the hardest part was just learning to live alone, learning to do so many things for herself. She really didn't miss Max per se, but she did miss the married life, the home and having "a man around the house." Sometimes she would joke and say, "I'm going to get me a six foot cardboard poster of Paul Newman to place in the corner of the kitchen, so that I can have a man around the house. That was about as much good as Max ever was anyhow."

What Beverly's story reminds us of is that the loss of a spouse can come in ways other than death. Beverly also reminds us that not all grief work is sad. Sometimes grief includes powerful feelings of anger, resentment and despair. These feelings must also be worked through if one is to be able to "let go" of the past and move on to the next phase of life.

Loneliness

The initial throes of grief are demanding, painful and horrible. Some people say that the first month is the worst. Pain and agony dominate our lives, consume our energy and take up most of our waking time and sometimes our sleeping hours. These are the times when family support is most crucial and useful. It is helpful having relatives and family present. They can carry us through the initial days and weeks, making decisions, completing chores, notifying relatives and taking care of some of the unpleasant chores that accompany a funeral and burial.

What most widowed people experience, however, is that family support gives way within a few days or weeks. Sooner or later, and usually it's sooner, the widowed person is left alone. Now we are really alone perhaps for the first time since our spouse's death. Now we feel the depth of our loneliness. Returning to that empty house, sleeping in the empty bed, setting a place for one at the dinner table—these are some of the little things, and there are many more as well, that rub salt in the wound of grief. These are the things that remind us that we are truly alone. Our pain reaches a new depth, an existential depth that rattles the very foundations of our soul.

Loneliness is the most difficult of the long-term problems of widowhood. The grief wound will heal in time, but loneliness is a mental state that will not heal. After grief is done, Dr. Feinberg says:

> There remains loneliness. This is a longer-range result, which is not susceptible to the same healing process. Loneliness is the reaction to the *absence of the valued relationship* rather than to the *experience* of the loss. Every other aspect of grief may subside as time goes on, but as long as no new relationship is formed to replace the one that is lost, loneliness continues.[9]

Loneliness is a condition of later life after our spouse dies. It is just a part of the nature of life. It cannot be fixed or "cured." It can be "cared" for, and caring does much to help widowed people cope with the loneliness.[10] But loneliness is not usually cured, except in forming a new love relationship. Some people will do that, but for most others in later life, especially women, that cannot or will not happen. They must learn to live with loneliness.

About a year after her husband's death, Bonnie had an experience wherein she really felt the pain of being alone. One day she was going down the stairs to put the laundry into the dryer, when she slipped on the bottom stair and fell on her back, twisting her foot. She was in pain, and could hardly move. Her first impulse was to call out, "Bob! Bob!" Then she remembered—there was no Bob. She was alone. She could not move. The worst pain of all, though, was the loneliness. She just lay there and cried, not just for the pain in her foot, but for the pain in her heart. It was a little frightening, too, when she reflected on it some days later. She could have been there for days before anyone would have discovered her plight. It was this incident that seemed to really crystallize so well how alone and potentially helpless she really was. There are probably many widowed people that can tell similar stories. Living alone is lonely and a little frightening.

Learning To Reach Out

Social isolation is slightly different than, but related to, the problem of loneliness. Social isolation is usually defined as being isolated from a social network of friends, family, work colleagues, etc. Most widowed people discover that they are both lonely *and* socially isolated after their spouse dies. Most widowed people discover that once they are widowed their social network changes dramatically. Many of their couple friends gradually cease calling or visiting. Associates of the deceased spouse, work colleagues, and friends also fade away in time. Perhaps they are uncomfortable because you remind them of their loss. Perhaps you remind them of their own potential mortality. Perhaps you are a threat to them somehow. For whatever reason, widowed people become more socially isolated with time.

Most widowed people try to socialize. They are told that they need to get out of the house. It is hard at first, because they are so used to doing things as part of a pair. It is hard going to restaurants alone, to movies by yourself, or to church and sit alone. These are awkward activities to do at first, and every time we do it, we are reminded again that we are alone. Yet, the advice-givers are correct. Our mental health does depend on how much we socialize, on how well we can rebuild a network of support for ourselves.

As the years pass, our circle of friends shifts more and more to people our own age and status. This is not entirely desirable, but other widowed people do understand our feelings more than most others. In time we may even relocate, giving up the larger family home for smaller quarters designed for a single person. If we relocate to a facility for the aged, we may re-experience the pain of being alone. We never wanted to be here—alone. It was never our wish to spend our older years without our life partner. We may wish that our spouse was here all the more. Being lonely is bad enough, "but to be old and lonely is the pits," as one friend of mine said recently. I would add, "Being old, lonely and poor is the absolute worst." This is the plight of many of our elderly citizens. Loneliness and social isolation are facts of life for the older single person. The loss of spouse is the event that ushers in this predicament, and from that point on we must learn to live with loneliness.

In spite of the fact that social isolation increases with age and dramatically increases after the death of our spouse, we must and can work hard at learning to reach out. Social support, family and friendships, even involvement in larger issues of the world, are important ingredients in staying youthful in the later years.[11] In fact I would argue, as does Eugene C. Bianchi, that this is *the* spiritual developmental task of late life, learning to stay involved.

> Elderhood, therefore, is not a time to withdraw from the world, but rather to make a special offering to fellow humans through a deeper involvement in the worldly sphere. We do not agree that "the last time is for oneself" . . . we have stressed the theme of an old age more fully committed to the great needs of humanity.[12]

Obviously not everyone stays active, nor can everyone, because of physical limitations, do so. (Being involved is as much a state of mind as it is a physical state.) Most people are just overwhelmed by the progressive losses of later life and prefer to gradually withdraw from life. Nevertheless, I believe that this is the primary spiritual task of later life and the task that is ushered upon us when our spouse dies. Learning to reach out, learning to stay involved in life, requires that we first learn to grieve well.

Learning Independence

One of the central themes that I hear from widowed people is that they must learn to be independent and self-reliant again. Moreover if they have never really been "on their own," then they must learn independence for the first time. There are hundreds of little things that we have relied on our spouse to do for us. Now we must do them all.

Most people who have been married a long time grow to be dependent on their spouse. This is part of the nature of marriage. Even the most independent of individuals usually grow more dependent as the years go by. We have become accustomed to being dependent, psychologically, financially, and even physically. Then when our spouse dies, we are suddenly without our usual source of support. Suddenly we are forced to be self-sufficient all over again. For some people that will be relatively easy. For others, that process will be much harder.

Olive cried with tears of frustration as well as loss. This was the fourth time that she had had the Buick in the shop for those squeaky brakes. It was so frustrating. She felt that she was being given "the run around." Yet she knew so little about cars. That was Truman's hobby. He used to keep the cars humming. "Now that he's gone," Olive complained, "I have to do all this myself and I don't know a darn thing about cars. God help me if I ever break down on the highway."

Learning to do things on our own can be one of the more difficult adjustments of widowhood. Whatever our spouse used to do for us, we must now do for ourselves (or at least arrange to get outside help). Did she wash clothes? Now you must learn to do it. Did he do the taxes every year? Now you must. Did she keep the gardens weeded? Now you must. Did he paint the house every summer? Now you must assume that assignment. Eventually, we will have to reduce our responsibilities, not expand them. But as long as we are able, we must assume new roles. We must become more self-reliant. We can do it if we take it easy and look upon it as a challenge. We may not be able to do these things as well as our spouse did, and that's okay too. We are learning.

For Jess money was one of those areas that Darlene had always taken charge of. He just gave her his paycheck every two weeks. He probably had not written a check in ten years. But now he had to learn the ropes. In fact now that she was gone, he had a strong urge to "put his life in order." He wanted to see the old tax returns and review the insurance policies and update his will. He wanted to get things settled, so the kids knew exactly what to do when he "passed on." In addition he knew that he would be living on a reduced income in the next few years. He had to start managing his money now.

Otherwise it wouldn't last. He didn't want to end up like his mother, poor and sick, in some state warehouse for the elderly.

"I've had a funny desire to put my house in order since Darlene died," he told me. "I guess I am preparing for my own death or something like that. I want to take inventory of my life, see what I got, and how long it can last me. If I live as long as my mother, I'll go broke—unless I learn to manage money."

"Will you?" I asked.

"Certainly. Old dogs can learn new tricks," he affirmed. "Just watch me."

Dependency is a word that has taken on negative connotations in our individualistic culture. Much of pop psychology which influences the media so thoroughly these days emphasizes the dangers of being overly dependent. We are told of the value of self-assertion, self-worth and "looking out for number one." One gets the impression that dependency is "a four letter word" and that we should all strive to be rugged individualists. Our theological perspective reminds us, however, that dependency, particularly on God and others, is desirable. [13] God has made us to be "people who need people." This is part of our human nature. True independence is probably impossible and certainly highly undesirable, from my point of view. Everyone learns to balance his or her needs for independence and dependence. When our spouse dies, we are forced to shift in the direction of independence. We must learn to live alone and do for ourselves and protect ourselves in ways that we have not had to do in previous years.

Avoid Making Idols

Most widowed people, particularly in the early stages of grief, cling to the memory of their beloved partner. They resist letting go. They may even idealize the lost spouse. If we do not grieve in a proper and timely fashion, then this tendency to idealize the deceased gets exaggerated. It turns into idolization, which works to block our natural grieving process and keep us stuck in the past.

Jean Stevenson, a forty-six year old woman, was married to a noted physician in the community, Dr. John Stevenson M.D. After Dr. Stevenson's untimely death, Jean seem to grieve well enough, but in time the grief did not subside. By two years after her husband's death, Jean, who actually preferred to be called Mrs. John Stevenson, had made a little shrine to her deceased husband in his former office/study. There were photographs, trophies and awards everywhere—from certificates of merit from the American Medical Association to the first place trophy at the local YMCA bowling tournament. It was all there. He had been a very popular and active man who made many friends and contacts in the medical community. When visitors came to visit Jean, she would show them all through "his study," like a tour guide in the museum, only she added tears at all the right spots. In time visitors came less often, but the shrine lived on.

I had the opportunity initially to talk with Jean's adult children, who expressed great concern for their mother's lack of resolution of their father's death. The children visited her less often now themselves. They were increasingly uncomfortable with their mother's "tour." In fact, they were beginning to resent what their mother was doing to their father. "We don't recognize the man mother has created," they told me one day. "Mom has turned dad into a saint or something. We hardly recognize him. To us he was an ordinary guy. He cussed and he had a bad temper, but he was our dad. But this fellow that she has plastered about the walls—that's not dad; that is some Greek god!" "Mom hasn't let dad go," one of the daughters continued. "She is still trying to keep him alive. I wish she would let him die. For God's sake, let him rest in peace."

Widowed people can, just like people grieving any loss, make what was lost into an false god. It starts with idealizing the beloved spouse. They gloss over his or her mistakes and faults. They remember the lovely, tender, wonderful moments. Now, all of this is normal enough. Everyone idealizes the departed, especially if one enjoyed a good relationship with the spouse. Yet if people get stuck there, then they have made their spouse into a mini-god. They have started to worship at the shrine instead of at the altar of the living God.

One way to get at the issue of idolatry is by examining the beliefs that inform one's operational theology. By so examining, we can often see clearly that an individual has constructed a theology that is based on a false god. Jean Stevenson was very consumed with her husband's success long before he died. She lived by the belief that "I am worthwhile because I am married to a successful man." Her identity was his identity. Her worth was in his success. She came to glorify in his success, as if it was her own. When John died, she never challenged that belief; she just rearranged it to read: "I am worthwhile because I *was* married to a successful man." So she continued to glory in his success. In fact in her grieving the story got more exaggerated.

Jean's story reminds us of another common belief, a more generalized belief, that many widowed people affirm. This creed reads: "The happiest time of my life was when I was married." Sounds innocent enough, doesn't it? Most of us, especially if we had good marriages, give assent to this credal statement. Yet, it can be a destructive belief if carried to the extreme. Such an assumption can prevent us from seeing the possibilities for happiness in the present moment. Surely in the midst of our grief, we have all said, "Life is meaningless now," or "There is nothing for me now," or "I cannot go on without him or her," and so on. But we did not get stuck there. We did not start to believe that salvation is found only in the past— or did we?

Fortunately, Jean Stevenson got some help for her idolatry, and through a process of therapy, individually and with her children, she was able to let go of her fierce loyalty to her husband. Her new life began to emerge when she was elected to the board of directors of the local community hospital. At first it was an honorary position, partly out of respect for her deceased husband, but in time she made the "calling" her own. She poured herself into fund-raising, community outreach programs and employee relations. She was a model board member, giving time and energy beyond all bounds.

She went on to live thirty years after her husband died. They were good years, filled with purpose, service to others and self-worth. When she finally "retired" there was a testimonial dinner at the hospital, not for Doc Stevenson's wife, but for Jean Stevenson: community leader, humanitarian and volunteer par excellence. She had reordered her life and her theology. Her operational creed now read, "I am worthwhile because I do worthwhile things." Not a perfect belief, but a whole lot more healthy than her former creed.

Each stage of life is valuable in its own right and the post-marriage stage of life can be valuable too. In many ways it may be the most valuable. God has a plan for each of us during this stage of our lives, just as God had purposes for each stage of our lives up to this point. We are still alive for a reason and we are alone for a reason. We need to find these reasons and "work out our salvation with fear and trembling" (Phil 2:12). The years we spent with our husband or wife were good years hopefully. The present years can also be good—maybe a different kind of good, but still good. In order for this goodness to emerge, we must first grieve.

Letting Go, Again

As we get older, it seems to be harder and harder to let go completely of past losses, and the loss of our spouse is one of the hardest losses to let go of. The loss of spouse does demand so many significant adjustments in our life style, roles and attitudes. It is a painful loss to grieve. It is so tempting to think that happiness can be found only by going backward, not forward. And so, while we do not make little shrines to our dead spouse, neither do we live fully in the present. We long for the past. The living God, however, is not in the past, but always pulling us toward a new life in the future. So, we must again let go—let go again, knowing that the invisible arms of the Almighty will support us and carry us forward to a new stage of our journey called life.

Notes

1. For example, see Thomas Bradley Robb, *The Bonus Years*, p. 65.

2. U.S. Bureau of the Census, "Marriage, divorces, widowhood, and remarriage by family characteristics: June, 1975," in *Current Population Reports*, Series P-20, No. 223 (Washington, D.C.: U.S. Government Printing Office, 1971).

3. Lynn Caine, *Widow: The Personal Crisis of a Widow in America* (New York: William Morrow and Co. 1974), p. 177.

4. Let me say that most women I have known can and do become more independent when they must. There is nothing inherently more dependent about the female nature compared to men, although I do think that there are other characteristics that are inherently more female.

5. See Chapter Two of Colin Murray Parkes, *Bereavement: Studies in Grief in Adult Life* (New York: International Universities Press, 1972).

6. The term "unexpected" refers to a subjective, relative experience. All but a very few of deaths are really unexpected, and even the expected deaths that come after a long illness have an element of unexpectedness in the end.

7. See Robert Jay Lifton, *Death in Life* (New York: Random House, 1967).

8. Women who are widowed between the ages of fifty and seventy-five only remarry 6.4 percent of the time (U.S. Census, 1977).

9. Dr. Mortimer R. Feinberg, Gloria Feinberg and John J. Tarrant, *Leavetaking* (New York: Simon and Schuster, 1978), pp. 239–240. The emphases are the authors'.

10. I am drawing on Henri J.M. Nouwen's distinction between care and cure. See his article, "Care and the Elderly," in Carol LeFevre and Perry LeFevre, editors, *Aging and Human Spirit*, pp. 323–328.

11. I recognize that there is a popular theory of aging, called the "disengagement theory," associated with the name Elaine Cummings, that argues that older people do naturally "disengage" from society as they age, and that this is normative. I would argue that is is typical, but not necessarily desirable.

12. Eugene C. Bianchi, *Aging as a Spiritual Journey*, p. 220.

13. Perhaps a better word, if we are describing normative theological conceptualization, is "inter-dependence." God has indeed made humans, in fact all of life, to be interdependent. Dependency is not necessarily a negative thing, but it is presented as such in much pop psychology.

Chapter 8

The Loss of Health

"So do not lose heart. Though our outer nature is wasting away, our inner nature is being renewed every day" (1 Cor 4:16).

One of the inevitable losses that everyone faces in later life is the gradual loss of health. All of us will experience this loss unless we die unexpectedly at an early age. For most of us there is no single, sudden loss of health. The loss of health is experienced as a gradual decline, peppered with many points of realization when we are keenly aware of what we have lost. Actually, we might say that the loss of health is really many losses, all strung together over the years. With each loss in health or realization thereof, we must learn to modify our life style to take into account our new limitations or ailments. Some of us make modifications easily. Others get caught up in denial or feelings of bitterness or despair. Dealing with the loss of health becomes a perpetual theme in the second half of life.

The First Experience of This Loss

As a part of my health maintenance program, I do a little jogging. In the process of participating in various running events in recent years, I have always noticed that the largest number of participants are always in the age range of forty to fifty-five years. The competition for medals among these categories of runners is fierce. Not too many younger competitors. Not too many older competitors. I suppose the older people are not there in large numbers because running gets to be an increasingly stressful sport for older bodies. The younger persons are not there in large numbers because they are still taking their health for granted. So, why are the middle-aged men and women there in force?

In almost every case where I have talked at length to middle-aged runners, I find that these people are unusually aware of the fragile nature of their health. Typically, they have some "horror story" that illustrates this point. The conclusion of the story is always, ". . . and that's what started me running." I have speculated therefore that middle age is about the time that many people first experience a loss in health. This loss is relatively minor, compared to the losses that will come later in life, but the novelty of this first loss has a powerful effect. It motivates some people to get involved in running in a very serious way.

This first loss or first awareness of loss is often a very powerful experience precisely because it is our first realization that our health is declining. There is an existential quality to this first loss of health that shakes the foundations of our life. Furthermore, how we react to this, the first health loss, often sets the pattern for how we shall respond (or did respond) to the many losses of health to follow. The first one sets the mold. We have a choice between facing reality and evasion. How we choose this time, more than in the times to follow, determines the direction of our spiritual journey.

The actual loss or realization of loss can occur in hundreds of ways, large or small. Some people experience this first loss in very dramatic ways. Perhaps they have a heart attack or develop a chemical dependency or lose a body part in an accident. Now they are forced to make radical adjustments in their life style, in their diet, in their daily routine, in their priorities and their attitudes. These adjustments will be preceded by some difficult emotional dynamics. Sudden losses do get our attention. They are hard to deny. Yet the sudden nature of the change can be overwhelming. Most of us will need time to process our feelings, change our attitudes and then modify our behaviors. If we have been caught by surprise, then these adjustments will take some time.

For most people this first realization of the loss of health usually comes in "smaller," more subtle ways. Can you remember when you first realized your body was declining? Perhaps you realized one Monday morning, as your muscles ached with pain, that you just can't play tennis once a month and expect to perform as usual. Or perhaps you have thrown your back out for the third time this year after trying to move furniture. Or perhaps your physician has just had a serious talk with you about your forty extra pounds or your high blood pressure. Or perhaps you've discovered that you are border-line diabetic and it runs in the family.

Typically, these kinds of changes first get noticed when we are in our forties or fifties. Yet it is hard to say exactly when and where this first realization of the loss of health comes. It is largely a subjective experience. Some of us can be very good at ignoring the many "clues" that our bodies offer us. We flee from the frightening feelings and implications embedded in those "clues." This is the first awareness of the loss of health.

Changes in Our Assumptions About Life

The experience of the loss of health is tied closely with our experience of our own finitude which is also a common theme during the mid-life years and beyond. It is related therefore to the loss of youth, which was discussed in Chapter Three.[1] We first experience our finitude not in any direct encounter with death, but in the bumping up against our own limitations. This realization of our limitations can be experienced in several areas of life during the later years. We might experience limits in our career, and/or in our finances, and/or in our emotional life, and, of course, in our health. The loss of health can be understood as a part of this larger experience of "bumping up against the limits" that becomes more common as we pass the midpoint of life.

Part of the uniqueness of the loss of health in the second half of life, as compared to the life's first half, is that these losses of health are now permanent in nature. Increasingly we are dealing with changes in our health that are permanent or semi-permanent conditions. Up to this point in our lives, our occasional physical limitations have been temporary in nature. We get sick and we get well. We break a leg and it heals. We are tired and we rest. We experience distresses in our bodies as temporary. We remember so well our mother's sweet assurance, "Tomorrow you'll be as good as new." Our operational belief about illness is that "this too will past." Most of us have never had to learn to deal with permanent limitations—until now.

The finality of these losses is new and challenges our basic assumptions about life and health. Initially most of us do not realize that this change has taken place. We respond to illness or limitations as if they can be fixed and then we can go on with life as usual. Unbeknown to us the rules of the game of life have changed.

Jim's experience with hypertension was like this. When his doctor first told him that his blood pressure was dangerously high, he was concerned. He had never had high blood pressure before, but he had read about the potentially dangerous effects of chronic high blood pressure in magazines and health journals. He was appropriately alarmed. Jim's first response was to try to cure it. He lost twenty pounds, began exercising daily and watched his stress levels. Sure enough the blood pressure went down. He fixed it—so he thought. Then over the months to follow, Jim again got busy at work and began to be less faithful with his new health habits. Two years later, at his regular checkup, the blood pressure was back up there again, as high as ever. Again he began exercising, and he again was able to lower the numbers. This time, however, he monitored the situation more carefully, almost scientifically. Jim noticed that as soon as he let up, even just a little, the blood pressure rose that next month. That's when it really hit Jim. A new realization began to surface in his consciousness: he wasn't ever going to cure his blood pressure problem. It was here to stay, for the rest of his life. The problem was permanent, final. This was a hard concept to get into his mind at first. He had to change his way of thinking about health, from viewing physical problems as temporary, to beginning to see them as permanent. Only as Jim made this conceptual change (I would say, change in operational theology) did his response to the blood pressure change too. To effectively deal with the blood pressure problem, his behavioral changes needed to be as permanent as the condition. He needed a response that matched the new reality.

Another of these operational beliefs associated with the loss of health that Jim's story illustrates is the assumption that our body will take care of itself. In the past when we were young, our body did take care of itself to a great extent. It developed automatically. It seemed to recover from illness or injury well enough. There was usually a parenting figure watching out for our body, of course. Nevertheless, for the most part, our bodies seemed to heal themselves. There seemed to be an underlying thrust toward health and growth.

Now post mid-life, the situation has changed. Our bodies do not automatically take care of themselves. In fact, we now see something quite frightening. We see that the natural inclination of the body is decline, not growth. If we just leave the body alone, as we always have done, it will not grow, nor will it even stay neutral; it will gradually decline. Think about it! Gradually we gain weight with increased age, do we not? Our blood pressure rises. Our arteries harden with each passing year. Our muscles become more weak and inflexible as we age. All this is "normal," as normal as growth was in childhood. Decay is inevitable, as inevitable as health was through the first half of life. "A new level of brokenness is experienced," writes Eugene Bianchi, as we realize the inevitability of this decline of health.[2] The trend is toward decline.

Linda passed her fortieth birthday in good spirits because she had gotten on an exercise "kick" about a year before. She did not feel old. In fact in some ways she was in the best shape of her life. Yet she could see that the directionality of her body's processes had changed. "Up to this point," she noted, "you can be lousy to your body and get away with it, but from here on, you must take care of it. Eat right. Exercise. If not, it's all downhill."

This realization is very hard for some of us to see, and when we do see it, our souls cry out with St. Paul that the whole creation is in "bondage to decay" and we long for the "redemption of our bodies" (Rom 8:21–23). It is a frightening prospect, this decay. Yet we must face it. It is the truth. Only if we realize that the ground rules of life have changed can we then begin to deal with our health constructively. Only then can we modify our attitudes, our theological assumptions and our life styles accordingly.

Another way of saying the same thing is that from here on we must be "pro-active" regarding our health. In the past we could afford to be "re-active" to health problems. When it broke, we fixed it; and "if it is isn't broke, don't fix it." Now we cannot afford to continue that response pattern. Actually, at this stage of our lives we can probably be as healthy as we have ever been if we work at it. We certainly do not need to be old and sickly. The difference is that now we must work at it. We must take responsibility for maintaining our health, because the rules of the game have changed.

Responses to the Loss of Health

Obviously there are many people who do not make this shift in attitude from a re-active to a pro-active stance toward their health. Just look around. There are many many people middle age and older who gain weight year after year, who smoke until it kills them, who seem to ignore their doctor's advice about diet even when their health problem is staring them in the face. These people are largely denying their loss of health.

Denial is probably the most common way of responding to the loss of health. The initial health losses are so gradual and subtle that it is relatively easy to go on pretending that we can do everything that we used to do. Other people cling to denial even after their bodies have started to dysfunction and even after their physicians have given them explicit instructions regarding how to treat their ailment. Denial can be fatal.

Many people respond to the loss of health, especially after repeated attempts to fix their problems, with despair. Such people seem to resign themselves to the gradual decline of their health. They seem to adopt a fatalistic attitude. Yes, they periodically make token efforts to bolster their health on a re-active basis, but their efforts are short-lived. They "believe" that they are fighting a losing battle, that in this life death is victorious. Such people are often helpless and passive and seem to be just waiting for their time. This despairing response to the loss of health is rare in the early years of later life, but it becomes increasingly more common as we observe people in later and later stages of life.

Another common response to the loss of health is anger and bitterness. It is such a shock to many people when they realize that their health is fading, that their bodies now require time and intentionality. Some people feel betrayed by their bodies. Some people feel estranged from their bodies. Their bodies used to be so predictable, so trustworthy. Most of us are not accustomed to having physical limitations. Anger and frustration can be a normal, emotional response to the loss of health.

Pamela was fifty-four years old when she was diagnosed as having irritable bowel syndrome. Actually, she had had digestive problems for the last ten years, but they were easy to ignore. It was simple enough to "cure" the immediate problem, but over the long term her doctor told her that she must watch her diet. No more spicy foods. No more coffee. No more onions. No more Mexican salsa. No more alcohol. It was interesting to counsel with Pam over the following three to five years and observe her cyclical pattern of denial and anger. She would follow her doctor's orders for a while and her digestive tract would be O.K. Then she would cheat a little bit—onions on a hamburger here, a few cups of coffee there—just "to prove that she could still do it." And sure enough, within the day she was crippled over with pain and rushing to the bathroom with diarrhea. Again she would get some medicine and work hard to calm down her bowels and stomach. A few months later, however, the pattern would repeat itself. This cycle actually went on for years. As Pamela described it, she felt angry, "cheated" that she couldn't eat the way she used to. She just couldn't believe that she could never drink a glass of wine again, and so she'd try again and again to prove reality different than it was. And again her body would prove to her that things had changed. She would accept it as true and then test it one more time. She would accept her condition, then in anger try to prove that it wasn't so. Eventually, as she learned to grieve and let go, she accepted her loss of health and made the necessary changes in her life style.

Health and Salvation

I have suggested that when grief feelings are not worked through, one of the results can be a kind of idolatry wherein the person comes to worship that which is lost. Such people become fixated on the lost object—in this case, health—and believe in their deepest souls that they can have it back and keep it forever if they just work hard enough. Or to put it differently, the false god promises the worshiper a kind of salvation—in this case perpetual health.

Have you known people who seem to have made an idol out of their health and its maintenance? I certainly have. They are found most often in health food stores, in health spas, in tanning salons and at the vitamin counters. There is nothing wrong with such measures when they are done within reason, but the "true believer" does not practice moderation. The idol's demands are total or nothing at all. They become preoccupied, even obsessed with their bodies. They can sound like hypochondriacs, but their problem is deeper than the need for attention that drives most hypochondriacs to talk incessantly about their symptoms. Health worshipers believe (and I use that word intentionally) that their salvation lies in the maintenance of their health. In fact the health worshiper comes to equate health with salvation. They are one and the same in the mind of the worshiper. The unspoken illusion is that if I can maintain my health in a perfected state, then death, decay and disease can be held at bay or at least controlled.[3]

Health worshipers can be any age. They are more obvious and numerous during the middle age years, because health does seem to be more controllable then. The lure of the false god is plausible here. This is the time when health can still be maintained, even with only a modest effort. Regardless of the age of the health worshipers, if we could examine their psyche we would always find unresolved grief feelings. They are not willing or able to face their feelings of loss about their declining health. Instead they flee into idolatry, hoping that by idolizing health, they will never have to face their own finitude.

Idolization cannot endure, because health, like all false gods, is temporary, finite and of "this world." In time one's health does decline, and then it becomes apparent to the once true believer that this god has failed. Idolatry fades in time. Perhaps it will be replaced with a new defense or more likely with despair. Or perhaps the former true believer will begin to deal with the feelings that he/she has ignored for so long. Then and only then is there an opportunity for that person to respond in faith and with realism.

This discussion of the idolatry of health raises several complex questions that cannot be addressed thoroughly in this chapter. One of the key questions goes something like this: "Where is the line between a pro-active health maintenance program and health worship?" This is a very tricky question for every person who both cares about his or her health and who also wants to live in the way of faith.

Unlike other losses of later life, the loss of health can be prevented or at least tempered with a pro-active program of health maintenance. More and more people, especially people in the later years, are "health conscious" and are taking steps to keep themselves in good health. This is largely a positive development, one to rejoice in. Yet when and where does health maintenance become health idolization? From my perspective the key variable is whether a person has dealt realistically with his or her grief feelings. Persons who have worked through their grief feelings can embrace a health maintenance program and keep it in perspective. At the other extreme are persons who enter a health maintenance program, usually in an obsessive mode, as a way of avoiding their grief feelings. As Christians, we believe that the body is good and that God wants all people to live in full health as long as possible. However, health is not an end in itself; it is a means to an end. The end is always salvation. The person of faith will keep his or her sights set of the larger goal of life's journey and not get lured into worshiping health no matter how attractive that altar might appear.[4]

Loss of Function

As we continue to age into the sixth, seventh and even eighth decades of life, the loss of health remains a constant theme. We must regularly deal with the little losses and declines that accompany each year. For many people, however, the next major time when the loss of health becomes a crucial issue occurs when they experience the loss of a major bodily function. The result of this loss is the first chronic condition or physical limitation. Examples of such losses would include the loss of sight, the loss of hearing, the loss of mobility and the loss of sexual function. We not only have the loss per se to deal with, but now we must learn to live with some permanent physical limitation.

Our response to a major function loss is probably not going to be too dissimilar from our response to the earlier occasions of loss, except for two things. First, our response is more colored by fear than anger. By now the cumulative effect of loss upon loss has taken its toll on us. Death seems closer to us now than it used to be. We have less energy to fight back and more easily slip into despair, covered over by a veneer of disgust. The loss of a major body function also means the loss of independence. We have not felt this secondary loss quite this sharply until now. This is a new wrinkle, a new challenge. This kind of loss of major bodily function is a frightening experience particularly for people who have valued their independence and self-sufficiency.

The Academy Award winning movie "On Golden Pond" was a wonderful study in aging, old age and inter-generational healing. Henry Fonda and Katharine Hepburn played the principal roles with the richness and intensity that only two great veterans of the theater could do. As the movie opens Norman Thayer and his wife Ethel are coming to the summer cabin in late spring, next to Golden Pond, where apparently they had spent many a previous summer. Now, however, Norman is approaching his eightieth birthday. He is struggling with his old age and declining health. His response is largely a not-too-subtle attitude of bitterness, sarcasm and denial. He simultaneously knows that he has health limitations, limitations that he did not use to have, and at the same time pretends that he can still work, fix doors, find directions and drive motorboats the way he used to. Ethel's responses are supportive and even upbeat, but also realistic.

In one particularly powerful scene Ethel encourages Norman to pick strawberries down by the Old Town Road instead of looking for "gainful employment" in the newspaper's want ads. Grudgingly, Norm takes the pail and proceeds down the path. With a wonderful piece of acting and camera work, we then see Norman get disoriented and confused in the woods and then progressively more frightened. He does not recognize where he is and cannot find the Old Town Road. He becomes panicky. He is frightened and momentarily lost. Finally, in what probably seems like an eternity to Norman, he finds his way back to the cabin with an empty pail in hand and the perspiration of anxiety dripping from his face. He jokes his way through the awkward conversation with his wife and the mailman regarding why he returned so quickly and without any strawberries.

Later, when he and Ethel are alone, he reveals why he returned so quickly from the strawberry search in a dialogue that goes something like this:

"You want to know why I came back so fast," he says in a hostile tone. "I got to the end of our land and I couldn't remember where Old Town Road was. I wandered away there in the woods. Nothing looked familiar. It scared me half to death. . . . That's why I came back, to your pretty face, so I could feel safe, where I'm still me." In obvious anguish and humility, he then sits down, with his head in his hands.

Ethel comforts him: "You're safe. You old fool. . . . Listen to me, Mister. You're my knight in shining armor. Don't you forget it. You're going to get back on that horse, me beside you, and away we go."

"You're a pretty old dame, aren't you?" responds Norm. "What are you doing with an old dotty s.o.b. like me?"

"I haven't the vaguest idea," she answers in obvious tones of grace and acceptance.

It's a wonderful scene. It portrays so well the terrible, frightening feeling of declining health and loss of function. The terror of the strawberry search reveals to us the intensity of Norman's anxiety that he normally covers over with sarcasm and disgust. The strawberry incident is clearly a concrete visualization of the larger, more pervasive struggle with old age that Norman Thayer is caught in. Feeling that you are losing your health evokes anxiety in all of us. Feelings of confusion, disorientation, anger and panic lie just beneath the surface. It is all there in one scene—so particular and yet so universal.

Loss of Independence

There is no escaping the gradual loss of independence that comes with each decline in our health.[5] When a person loses a major bodily function, like sight or hearing, the dependency becomes very obvious and very real. Now the impaired person must learn new skills that perhaps he or she has never learned or has not practiced since childhood. All of the daily routines must be relearned, this time "with one hand tied behind your back." If we cannot walk, then we must learn to use a wheelchair or crutches. If we cannot hear, then we must make adjustments in communication. If our bladder cannot function, then we must learn to use an artificial one. If we cannot drive, then we must learn to use public transportation or to rely on others to get us to the market or the doctor or the bank. If one is living alone, then these adjustments are all the more difficult.

One of the results of a loss of a major body function and the corresponding loss of independence is a move from an independent living situation to a semi-independent or total-care living environment. This change of residence is not an easy change in its own right and might be experienced as a significant loss by some individuals. It is a transition that often confirms and/or even facilitates our loss of independence.

Bernice L. Neugarten, a gerontologist, has categorized the "new" old age into three parts: "the young old," "the old" and "the old old."[6] This distinction is based on the degrees of a person's relative health/independence rather than on chronology. People who can still live independently, who can still maintain an active life, perhaps working part-time and who need but routine medical care, fall into the category of "young old." The "old" need semi-independent living situations, where some routine support functions, like meal preparation, are provided and where medical care is easily available. The third stage of people, "the old old," must have full-time medical care and are largely unable to live independently due to their health limitations. These "stages" are not always neatly divided. Some people might go back and forth between several stages before transitioning to the next stage of residential care.

Each of these changes in the relative independence of a person's living situation may involve a change in residence. Many homes or residential communities for the aged cater to one level of need or another and require that the resident "move on" when he or she has passed into another phase of need. The most desirable living situations, however, are those residential communities that have all three levels of care available on the same campus. This arrangement allows people to pass from one level of care to another with the least disruption in their lives, and if necessary this arrangement also allows them to alternate between levels of care. The general rule of thumb is to try to maintain the most independence possible without endangering one's health. A sense of independence does much to help us maintain a positive attitude toward life.

When dealing with this difficult subject of declining health and independence/dependence, there is no substitute for advanced planning. The more we can anticipate our future health limitations and make plans accordingly, the easier time we will have with these transitions when they arrive. Planning ahead is possible only if we have dealt with our feelings about our present and future losses in health. If we deny those inevitable changes, we will avoid making plans and probably, when the time comes for a necessary relocation, the decision will be made *for us* rather than *by us*.

Florence was one of the wise, forward-planning people. When she was in her sixties and still in fairly good health, she lived alone in an apartment complex for "senior citizens." It was a nice apartment in a very pleasant location. There was no reason to move, but one day she put her name in for the new Senior Citizen Towers that was being constructed down the block. "Why?" I asked her. "Why would you want to leave this nice cozy place?"

"The stairs," she noted. "I won't always be able to get up those stairs when I get older. I need to get into a place that has elevators. And I'll want a smaller place then, one that I can manage easily."

She was anticipating the loss of health that was to come. She had been around old people often enough so that she knew what was ahead of her—and she was right. She did become less mobile over the years that followed. Her bad foot became harder and harder to walk on, but long before that happened, she had moved into an efficiency apartment in the new Senior Citizen Towers where she did not have stairs to contend with. She was one person who not only accepted the reality of declining health, but actually planned for it in a realistic way. Her response was not denial or despair, but a realistic appraisal of her future and appropriate action. She prepared herself, and by preparing herself she was able to make her loss of health a non-problem. She passed through the transition from independent to semi-independent living with ease. She was able to spend her time and energy on more important matters during these years than on worrying about how she was going to negotiate the stairs each day.

Transcending the Body

The spiritual challenge that awaits us all as our health declines from minor losses to major limitations is to increasingly transcend the body. This is not an easy assignment. We are accustomed to equating ourselves with our bodies. If my body is sick, I say "I'm sick." Or if my body is well today, I say, "I feel fine today." We are not accustomed to separating ourselves from our bodies. We are naturally wholistic. Yet many older people, especially spiritually sensitive people, tell me that as they get older they are able to distinguish themselves more and more from their bodies. They begin to realize that their essence, their true being, is not limited to their physical condition. They realize that their mind, their spirit and their personality can be still very healthy and very alive, even while their body is declining in vigor. We might even say that such people have discovered their soul. They realize that their true being is not their body, but their soul. By shifting perspectives on themselves in this way, they are able to increasingly transcend the body's limitations.

Obviously this kind of spiritual maturity that I describe is rare among the general population. Most people do not seem to rise above their ailments, except on momentary occasions. It is hard to transcend the body. In fact many older people develop what Robert C. Peck calls "body preoccupation."[7] They become increasingly absorbed with their body and its subtle aches, pains and changes. We have all met older people who seem to talk on endlessly about their last surgery or who can describe in detail yesterday's bowel movement or who despair at length about their declining strength. Obviously the bodily hurts and our physical limitations can cause us great pain and frustration. It is hard to transcend pain. It is easy to become absorbed with one's body over the passing years.

Transcending the body is a modern way of talking about what historically religious people called the art of suffering. We all suffer as our bodies decline. Some of us will even be in chronic pain or be permanently limited in what we can do. Suffering is a regular companion in old age (and sometimes even in middle age). The spiritual challenge before us at this stage of life's journey is learning to suffer well. We are called by God to learn to rise above our pain, our limitations and our sufferings, to see life and ourselves as larger than our physical existence. We are called by God to focus our life on the things of the spirit and to stay focused here even as "our outer nature is wasting away."

Erik H. Erikson, the dean of life-span psychology, has himself passed on into old age. His latest book, *Vital Involvement in Old Age*, which he co-authored, reflects on the nature of the later years.[8] He too suggests that learning to transcend the ills of old age is difficult, but that "staying active" is the best way to transcend physical limitations. By active, he does not mean just physical activity, but "vital involvement." One can be "involved" even from a wheelchair. To the extent that we stay involved in the world, says Erikson, we shall transcend our physical limitations. Obviously others can help us greatly in this regard and can lure us away from the natural tendency toward self-absorption and bodily preoccupation.

If you recall the rest of that movie, "On Golden Pond," you will remember that Norman's daughter (Jane Fonda) leaves her thirteen year old stepson-to-be with Norm and Ethel for a month, while she and his father travel elsewhere. As the story unfolds we see the interplay between generations, young adolescent and old man. By the time the movie ends, Norman is no longer the bitter, despairing old man that he was at the start of the summer. All of his bodily ailments are there, of course, but his spirit is different. In my terminology, Norman has momentarily "transcended his body" and begun to focus on the things of the spirit: relationships, sharing, enjoying and being. It is a powerful argument for the value of inter-generational contact and relationships. He experiences again that the real Norman is not his body, but his spirit.

Learning to suffer well or transcend the body is not easy.[9] It does require a very subtle but important change in our self-understanding. We need to come to see ourselves more and more as spiritual beings, not as earthly creatures. Our body, like everything which is of "this world," is finite, temporary and fragile. Our real worth lies in our spirit, our soul, our personality. To put it in different terms, most of our lives we have valued *doing* modes—producing, accomplishing, making, having. Now, we need to come to value *being* modes—understanding, sharing, knowing.[10] For most of our lives we have valued ourselves and been valued for what we produced, how we looked, what we owned or what we made. Now God's challenge to us in our old age is to shift modes of valuing: from having to being. If we do so, we can learn to value ourselves for who we are. We can increasingly learn to nurture our souls even while our bodies are declining.

The Value of Being Handicapped

Everyone should know at least one handicapped person. Charlotte was crippled in an automobile accident at age seventeen and has been on crutches ever since. I have had the privilege "to walk" (literally and figuratively) with Charlotte for many years as her friend and counselor and pastor. I have listened to her despair at being "deformed" and her frustration at being helpless. I have listened to her anger at how "people stare at my legs, not because they're pretty but because I'm a freak or something." I have grieved with her at the life that might have been. I have listened to her questions whether she would ever marry or could ever hope to cope with children. Yet I have also admired her courage as she pushed her limits again and again. I have been instructed by her humility and gratitude toward what health she does have. And I have seen what a genuinely beautiful person, spiritual person, she has become over the years. Everyone should know at least one handicapped person, especially one like Charlotte.

There is a handicapped person in your future: you! Handicapped persons are dealing in the present moment with what you and I will have to deal with later. Sooner or later each of us will become handicapped in one way or another. Sooner or later each of us will have to deal with one or several major losses in our health. Then we will travel down the same path that the handicapped person currently walks. Then we will know their pain, frustration and sufferings. Perhaps if we could learn from them now, whatever our age, we would be better prepared for our own future.

Handicapped persons teach us that life is more than a body. They demonstrate the truth of all of the great religions that the things that make us truly human and truly divine are not physical qualities. They are qualities of the Spirit. St. Paul listed a few of these qualities: love, joy, peace, patience, kindness, goodness, faithfulness, gentleness, self-control (Gal 5:22). Jesus listed a few more: meekness, peacemaking, purity of heart, mercy, hunger for righteousness, suffering in a right cause (Mt 5:3–10). Neither of them mentioned physical beauty or even physical health. The qualities that save us do not include the shape of our bodies.

Handicapped persons also can teach us how to suffer and how to rise above bodily limitations. Sometimes pain cannot be fixed, nor can all limitations be conquered. Most of us will have to deal with pain and limitations, at first in minor ways and later in major ways. We will learn new meanings for the word "courage." Either we will rise above our limitations and learn to live with them or we shall sink to new lows of despair, bitterness and helplessness. The choice depends largely on the strength of our courage.

In a sense, then, a handicap or a loss of health can become a gift. It never starts out that way. Initially it is a horrible loss. If through the loss, however, we can learn to nurture our spiritual qualities and learn the art of suffering well, then we will have transformed our loss into a gain. We will have grown in and through our loss. We will have risen above our loss precisely by not letting it defeat us, but by letting it propel us forward into a more advanced stage of human existence. Admittedly, not everyone makes such a major leap forward. Neither have some human beings made it past a Sunday school theology. Yet, the loss of health in later life, as horrible as it seems, can be the opportunity for growing toward an even greater level of spiritual maturity.

Notes

1. All of the losses discussed in this book are interrelated. One loss may trigger and/or reinforce another loss, which in turn may make us aware of a still third pending loss.

2. Eugene C. Bianchi, *Aging as a Spiritual Journey*, p. 143.

3. Another way to look at this idolatry theologically is as an ultimate reliance on human effort instead of on God's grace. It is the ultimate form of earning your own salvation. Health worshipers practice this kind of reliance on technology and one's own efforts to "earn" the promised salvation.

4. For a more sophisticated discussion of the interrelationship of health and salvation, see James N. Lapsley, *Salvation and Health: The Interlocking Processes of Life* (Philadelphia: Westminster Press, 1972).

5. The loss of independence actually takes many forms besides physical limitations. There is also the loss of independence that comes from reduced income, and there is a kind of emotional dependency that comes with increasing years.

6. She first made this distinction in "Age Groups in American Society and the Rise of the Young-Old," in *Annals of the American Academy of Political and Social Science,* vol. 415, 1974, pp. 187–98.

7. See Robert C. Peck, "Psychological Developments in the Second Half of Life," in Bernice L. Neugarten, editor, *Middle Age and Aging,* pp. 88–92.

8. Erik H. Erikson, Joan M. Erikson and Helen Q. Kivnick, *Vital Involvement in Old Age* (New York: Norton, 1986).

9. Admittedly it is a paradox: valuing ourselves more as spiritual beings and staying involved in the world. The inner focus and outer focus can and do go together, because at the deepest levels of our souls we are all linked to one another, to the earth and to God.

10. See Henri J.M. Nouwen and Walter J. Gaffney, *Aging: The Fulfillment of Life* (Garden City, New York: Image Books, 1976).

Chapter 9

The Loss of Identity

"But whatever gain I had, I counted as loss for the sake of Christ" (Phil 3:7).

"Who am I?" has become one of the most important existential questions of modern times. The quest for identity is no longer just a task of the adolescent, but a lifelong theme for most adults. It forms the cornerstone of the modern psyche. Yet our identity is built largely upon our roles and our emotional attachments to places, things and people. We define ourselves by our roles and by who and what we love. In the second half of life we begin to lose most of the roles and attachments that had undergirded our identity. Now we begin to feel a new kind of loss, one that grows out of the other losses and yet is also a separate loss in its own right. We begin asking ourselves again and again during the later years of life, "Who am I?" "Who am I—now that I am no longer a parent?" Or "no longer a worker?" Or "no longer a spouse?" Or "no longer even a whole person?"

Identity in a Changing Society

The concept of identity is a relatively new term in the history of western civilization. The term was largely unheard of prior to World War II, although surely the experience was described in other ways. Erik Erikson is generally given credit for coining the term "identity crisis," which rocketed the concept of identity into our every day consciousnesses.

What Erikson suggested was that an identity crisis occurred in every person during late adolescence, when he or she began trying to pull away from the family of origin. It was a normal developmental event. The main task of these years, suggested Erikson, was to form a "subjective sense of an invigorating sameness and continuity."[1] Adolescents find this sense of identity by testing out various roles, values, beliefs and world views, and receiving feedback from others. In time the young person comes to settle in with a sense that "This is the real me!" If a person does complete this task, then he or she is well prepared to proceed on into adulthood and its developmental stages. However, if adolescents fail to establish a sense of identity, then they experience role confusion, a confusion that will trap them perpetually at this stage of life. Erikson argued that this identity crisis was present in all cultures and peoples, but that the particular shape or intensity of the crisis depended on the culture and the individual involved.

The term "identity crisis" and the concept of identity has caught on in our society in a way unforseen even by Erikson. The term is now broadly employed by laypeople and scholars alike to describe a common experience. It seems as though everybody is having an identity crisis these days! Why do you suppose this is so? The concept seems to have resonated with something deep within us, within our common experience as persons living in the late twentieth century in western culture.

The quest for identity has become a theme of modern times. In fact some writers have suggested that identity crisis has become *the* main psychological problem of our times.[2] In that regard it is interesting to note that the problem of identity has become such an important issue in our modern culture that the American Psychiatric Association has actually catalogued a "new" type of mental illness, called an "identity disorder." The central feature of this disorder is "subjective distress regarding inability to reconcile aspects of self into a relatively coherent and acceptable sense of self."[3] Some of the areas of confusion might include: long term goals, career choices, friendship patterns, sexual orientation, religious identification, moral values and group loyalties. The DSM III clearly places identity disorder as a illness originating in adolescence, but I am sure that most adults feel as though they too have an identity disorder from time to time. Problems of identity have become a psychological feature of our times and our culture.

What is clear is that establishing and maintaining an identity is partly a social and even a cultural experience. It is not something we do in isolation. It is not something that is just psychological in nature. Social and cultural factors make it easier or harder for individuals in that society to find a sense of identity. Indeed individuals in more traditional, stable cultures seem to be able to find a sense of identity easier. Individuals in rapidly changing, pluralistic societies tend to have a more difficult time finding themselves. Perhaps this was why Alex Haley's book *Roots* and the related television mini-series seemed to touch so many chords both within the black community and in the larger culture. All of us modern people have, to some extent, lost our roots and therefore a sense of who we are. The plight of modern people, to a greater or lesser extent, is trying to find an identity in a culture that no longer offers the usual givens upon which identity is built.

This plight, however, is not too dissimilar from the plight that many individuals feel in the later years of life. Here too, many of the usual "givens upon which identity is built" have been stripped away. In a sense then there is a parallel between the rapidly changing culture of the last one hundred years and the experience of rapid change during the latter half of life. Each of these experiences in social and cultural instability makes it more difficult for the individual to find and keep a firm sense of identity.

What Is Identity?

What do we mean by identity exactly? Identity is simply a coherent sense of self. It is an awareness of knowing who and what we are, even while moving in and out of differing roles and life stages. The concept is then both sociological and psychological. It is something that we work out socially with the outside world and it is something that we process internally.

First, identity and identity formation is inseparable from our social roles. We define ourselves by our roles. We say, "I am a mother," or "a florist," or "an Englishman," or "a widow." The society shapes our identity for us by defining these roles and the behavioral expectations for each role. The identity of the mature person, however, should not limited to any single role. The individual is a collection of his or her many roles, but, even more than that, our identity should really be more than the sum total of all of our roles. Our identity, or the identity of a healthy person, should transcend our many roles, thus giving us a sense of "sameness and continuity" over the course of our lifetime, as well as over the scope of roles we might play in the course of a single day, week or month. Conversely, psychologically unhealthy persons have no strong sense of self beyond their roles and/or have defined themselves too exclusively by a single role.

Identity also has an internal or psychological side that is separate from but interrelated to the social dimension. Attachments are a way of describing this internal dimension. Attachments, as the reader will recall, include any thing, place or person that we emotionally attach ourselves to. We attach ourselves to very important persons, like our spouse, parents, children. We attach ourselves to friends, colleagues, neighbors. We can attach ourselves to places, home towns, schools, favorite possessions. The human tendency to form emotional bonds is universal and inevitable. It is part of our survival mechanism and it is related to our capacity to love. It is also one of the key ways of defining ourselves. We define ourselves by our attachments, or, to put it differently, our identity reflects our attachments—either way. By examining what I am bonded to, you can understand who I am and how I define myself. Our identity is derived from our attachments.

Whether we describe identity in terms of roles or in terms of attachments or both, it is clear that we build our identity on things that are potentially changeable. Social roles and emotional attachments change, most notably in the second half of life. What then happens to our identity?

Identity in Later Life

While Erikson argued that the primary locus of the identity crisis was in adolescence, it was clear that the issues raised by the identity crisis do not limit themselves to adolescence.[4] In recent decades, for example, there have been many people who have talked of the identity crisis of middle age, or "middlescence."[5] There are other writers who have described the identity confusion that widowed people experience following the death of their spouse.[6] In fact identity themes have surfaced in each of the major losses described in this book. Each loss brings with it a "mini" identity crisis, calling us to answer the question "Who am I . . . now that I am no longer a mother . . . or an engineer . . . or a young man . . . or a healthy person?" Each loss brings with it a change in our identity. Thus part of our grief process includes or should include a coming to terms with our lost identity.

David was a "child of the 1960's," so he said, but today at age forty-three he finds himself as a senior vice president of a large diversified manufacturing company. Now he wears pin-striped business suits to work every day and reads the *Wall Street Journal* on the commuter train. When David was a young man he wore blue jeans, marched in Washington, and swore against the evils of the "industrial military complex." In therapy David talks about the distress he feels between the two sides of his life.

"Part of me wants to go back to a college environment, maybe to do that doctorate in sociology that I never did . . . just throw in the towel on corporate climbing. Who needs it? . . . But I know that that is a bit of dreaming, a longing for my past, my youth. I know I'm no longer an idealistic college student, but I still want to be. I've changed and yet I haven't changed. Or maybe I haven't caught up with the changes that have gone on within me."

David's awareness of his loss of youth forces him to rethink who he is, who he has become, and, by implication, who he shall be.

Sally is twenty-five years old, married with two young children, and lives on the east coast where her husband's company sent them. Recently she was home for the holidays, visiting her parents in Iowa. They all were enjoying the visit as they often did. "It is fun watching my parents grandparent the children," she noted. "It gives you a wonderful perspective on your own childhood, and my parents do seem to enjoy being parents.

"You know what I noticed, really for the first time, was how much mom and dad address each other as 'mother' and 'father.' 'Would you pass me the potatoes, mother,' Dad might say. 'You're looking very handsome today, father,' Mom would say.

"I suppose it's a carry-over from when they mothered and fathered me and my brothers. Then it was always 'Go ask your mother' or 'Wait until your father gets home.' But now it seems out of place. Yes, they are still my parents and all, but *to each other* they are first and foremost husband and wife, lovers and friends.

"Well, you know, I actually said something to them about this, and they agreed with me. I guess they just needed someone to point it out to them. It kind of became a joke for the rest of the visit. I would correct them every time they referred to each other as 'mother' or 'father.' It was good to do something liberating for them."

Sally helped her parents change some of the last residue of their lost roles as "mother" and "father." Theirs was a subtle but important shift in identities. Fortunately, her parents were secure enough with their former identities as "husband" and "wife," as "lovers and friends," that they could return to those roles/identities easily. They just needed a little help.

Similar dynamics are often operative when people retire. At first it gets hard to know how to answer the question "Who are you?" or "What do you do?" (which is a disguised way of asking, "Who are you?"). "I used to say, 'dentist,' " notes retired Dr. Johnson. "Then I would catch myself and say, 'former dentist.' Then I got to really thinking about it. I'm so much more than just a dentist or a 'has been' dentist. I am a person, a husband, a Catholic, a Republican—and maybe, just maybe, I'll become a part-time politician or cabinet maker or resident mystic." What a wonderful attitude! The loss of an identity does open the door to an opportunity for some new roles, as long as one is sufficiently secure enough to let go of the past.

With each loss of later life, there is also a corresponding loss of identity. As we age, we are regularly losing pieces of our identity, which may or may not be replaced with new pieces. For some people this will not be a problem. They have formed an identity that transcends their many roles or is filled with so many roles and attachments that they can lose portions without losing their whole sense of self. What of the person, though, who has a fragile identity or an identity built upon a single role, as more and more people seem to do in large metropolitan areas? Such people will have a much more difficult time adjusting to the losses of later life. They will experience a significant and persistent loss of identity. Their grief will be more painful, precisely because they are losing something more than the obvious. They are losing a piece of themselves.

Loss of Home

In addition to the losses described earlier in this book, all of which involve an identity theme, there are a couple of other specific losses that also seem to fit into this loss of identity experience. One of these losses is the loss of home or homestead.

Most of us who live in urban or suburban areas do not easily appreciate the deep roots that some people can attach to their home and to "the land." In smaller communities or in rural communities, it is not uncommon for several generations of a family to have been born and raised in the same home or on the same land. People say "That's the Taylor house" or "the Wheeler farm," because some Taylor or some Wheeler has lived on that land for as long as anyone can remember.

When a person grows old, however, and the spouse is dead, and the children have moved away, and then health fades, there comes a time when he or she may have to move out of the cherished family home. Usually this "final" relocation is into a health care facility or a child's home where the older adult can be cared for more fully and lovingly. The loss of their home can be a difficult loss for many. People often have deep emotional attachments with their home.

Ethel was one such person. Her pastor told me about Ethel and the difficulty she experienced in moving from her home of forty-seven years. She and her husband built the home when they were "young kids" fresh out of high school. They planted the back acre and added a room later when the family grew bigger. Altogether they raised five children in their home. In recent years Ethel has lived alone in this big house, which is somewhat distant from town. She has fallen several times and her growing arthritis was making it difficult for her to care for herself. Karen felt strongly that it was time for her mother to move into a home for the aged, and there was one near her home in St. Louis that was perfect. There was just one problem—Ethel didn't want to move. The pastor who was involved in trying to talk to Ethel remembers some of the conversation.

"This is my home. Charles and I built this place. I know every nook and cranny. I have painted each wall a dozen times. The stain over there on the rug is from when Jack was sick as a baby, and those marks on the wall are from measuring the children's heights, and the apple tree out back was put in when our Inky (their family dog) died. It's all here, pastor, my whole life. I feel at home here. This is where I belong, not in some small noisy apartment in a city.

"You have a lot of memories here, wonderful memories. It's a hard place to leave," the pastor responded.

"What would happen to me there? It wouldn't be the same."

"Or you wouldn't be the same?" he inquired, "Is that what you fear? You know, you really wouldn't stop being yourself. You'll take that with you—the memories, the furniture, the pictures, your faith."

"You're so kind, pastor," she said as only a women in her ninth decade can say to a minister half her age. "It's hard to leave behind all of this. It's so much a part of me."

"You know, the Lord God asked Abraham to get up and leave his home one time. He didn't even tell him where he was going, only that he had to go and that he would go with him. I have often thought of how frightening that must have been for Abraham, who was just about as old as you are now."

"Did Abraham go?"

"Yes, Abraham went," the pastor smiled. "He went because he knew that where he was was not as important as whom he was with. You might say that he was a pilgrim, moving from place to place, never settling too long at any one place, lest he forget that his ultimate home is beyond this world."

"I guess God wants me to be a pilgrim too—but I don't like it much."

The pastor reported to me that Ethel did go to that "home" for the aged. It was not an easy transition for her, but the image of the pilgrim seemed to help some. "It's a good image," noted the pastor. "After all, we are all pilgrims in this life and periodically we must pick up and go."

What is clear from this example is that moving out of a long-time home is more than the mere loss of a house. It is a loss of a sense of roots, a sense of history, maybe even a sense of place. We humans seem to need those kind of places, places where we know who we are, sacred places. Places help anchor our identities. We better know who we are when we are there. In later life, however, we are regularly invited to pick up and go, to leave behind some of our roles, our identities, even our roots. Life in the later years is definitely a journey and we all must become pilgrims.

Loss of Our Generation

Another loss that most people experience in later life which also seems to fit this theme of the loss of identity is the loss of one's own generation. By "generation" I mean peers, friends, siblings—everyone of a given generation. As we pass through the second half of life, we notice that our peers begin to die with increasing frequency. At first, they are distant events—a movie star who dies in her fifties. It's a random accident. "How tragic," we note. "She was just a young woman." Then with each passing year, we notice more deaths among peers. They are no longer distant figures, but now people we've known personally, sometimes even closely. Perhaps our best friend dies, our college roommate, the maid of honor in our wedding, our confidant or our work colleague. If we live a long time ourselves, we will experience the deaths of many of these friends, peers, colleagues and siblings.

People who have studied old age say that this "passing on" of one's friends is a critical adjustment issue in later life. Friends are a very important piece of our mental health support system. We need our friends, especially if we live alone and have already lost our spouse. As our friends slip away, we can increasingly become more isolated, more lonely and more despairing. Many gerontologists have talked about the importance of making new friends, especially younger friends, as we age. We need some friends that can provide continuity in our support system. This is yet another argument for the value of inter-generational contacts. A few younger friends can help us experience social support when so many of our peer-aged friends are dying or becoming less able to support us.[7] There is much to be said for cross-generational friendships.

Wilma is a very talkative, delightful person of seventy-eight years. She resides in a retirement community near my home. We have talked some in church and over tea. She began to focus my attention on this loss in a series of conversations which I have reconstructed here.

"When Jack Benny died," she began, "that did something to me. There was something about his death that seemed to sadden me terribly. Then there was Jimmy Cagney, and I saw where Al Landon died the other day. These are people that I grew up with. I saw their movies. I voted for them. I identified with their lives. We shared the same planet for a period of time. They are my peers, my generation—that's it, it feels as though my generation is passing on before my eyes. There are fewer and fewer people left my age anymore.

"I'm just about the last of my family alive. I had seven brothers and sisters. Can you believe that? We lost James in the war and then Margaret died rather young, of cancer. Now I'm seventy-eight, and my brother, he's seventy-four, I think. That's all—just us two. We call each other, my brother and I, and talk about old times. No one else quite understands my life the way he does. He lived it with me.

"I've got plenty of children and grandchildren, but it's not the same. There is something about the passing of your own generation of family that makes you feel alone.

"Sometimes I talk with Mrs. Artress down the hall about the Depression and she hardly knows what I'm talking about. She was just a baby then. I mention 'Hooverville' and I have to explain it to her.

"You know, I think I have lived long enough, pastor. This is no longer my world. I don't feel at home here anymore. I don't understand the way people do things these days—the lack of regard for others, the drugs, crime and the government scandals. I even feel funny about church sometimes—it's too loose. Sometimes I wonder what the world will become after me.

"Maybe it's just time for me to move on. I know more people in heaven now then I do on earth. Almost all of my family is there now. Maybe it's time for me to go too."

Wilma has described so well this feeling that I call the loss of our generation. As we move on in the later years, we feel increasingly estranged from the world around us, from the "times." We have this sense that we are out of sync with the age, that we have lived too long.

Almost every older person can identify with Wilma's feelings regarding the progressive passing on of friends, same-generation relatives and colleagues. However, this loss of friends does not have to be as gloomy or as depressing an experience as Wilma makes it. Some older people who have remained active and involved in the world seem to delight in the changes around them and don't have that same sense of not being at home anymore. They look forward to living longer just to see what amazing things will happen next. Much depends on how flexible we are mentally. Can we adjust mentally to new ideas, new ways of doing things? If we have been or are mentally flexible, then we can approach life with ease and adjustment. If we have been or are mentally rigid, then it is harder to adjust to change. Life seems to be passing us by. Or to put it differently, much depends on how flexible our identity is and where/how we have grounded our identity. If we have over-identified with our generation, then it becomes harder to adjust when our generation passes on. When our generation moves on, then we feel, like Wilma, that we should move on too. But if we have formed an identity that is trans-generation or based on other attachments and images, then we may not have that same sense of loss. We may be able to grieve more easily and thereby live more hopefully.

Clinging to Lost Identities

One of the stereotypes of old age is that of mental rigidity. We tend to think of old people as conservative, as persons who resist new ideas, who cannot change, who are inflexible and who are "stuck in their ways." This view of old people is a stereotype and a dangerous one in that it can easily become prescriptive in nature, not just descriptive.

People age, of course, in a great varieties of ways. Some people do become more mentally rigid with the passing years, but many other people do not. Probably the individual's personality and personal mental history is more of an influencing factor in determining how well they will age than any innate tendency toward rigidity.[8]

Yet at another level, there is some truth couched in this stereotype that needs to be explored. Every person, as he or she ages, wrestles with a "choice" between mental flexibility and mental rigidity. It is one of the crucial issues in determining how well people will age.[9] Persons who drift toward greater mental rigidity age faster.

They seem old. They are old thinking. Conversely, people who can maintain a mental flexibility seem younger. Mental flexibility means being open to new ideas, being willing to learn and be corrected, being willing to change when necessary and being willing to grow. If we can consciously maintain mental flexibility, even as our bodies age, we shall remain young—mentally, emotionally, and spiritually.

Why might older people become mentally rigid? Is it really an "innate tendency" or is it a reaction to something else? I would argue that it is the latter. There is nothing inevitable about becoming mentally rigid or conservative in old age. I have known enough "young" thinking older people to believe that mental rigidity is not inevitable. Nevertheless, I admit it does appear that most older people do become more rigid with each passing year. This trend could be understood as a function of loss and idolatry. We become more rigid mentally, precisely because we feel that our identities are slipping away. Our world is changing and change is frightening. What do we do? We cling all the harder to those things that we feel certain about, our beliefs, our identities, our values. The more we feel the world changing, the harder we cling. Instead of dealing with our feelings of fear and grief, we deny the feelings. We run from them—in the opposite direction—toward greater rigidity. The psychological term is reaction formation. The theological term is idolatry. The more we feel our identities slipping away, the more we cling to them.

Mental rigidity is, simply put, a reaction to ungrieved losses, to unfaced feelings of sadness and anger. Mental flexibility, which is one of the characteristics of youth, is possible only when we grieve our losses, in particular our losses of identity. Only when we have emotionally let go are we free mentality to embrace a new idea and to change. If we want to stay young, mentally young, we need to regularly grieve the losses of identity that happen to us. That is a hard assignment, one that few people actually do well, but in my opinion it is the only way to stay young.

Becoming More Like Ourselves

Several people that I have talked with have described the experience of the progressive losses in later life as a type of "stripping away." The image is an apt one, one that seems to capture the dynamic for many people.

We used to think of ourselves as a young person with all of the trappings that go with youth. Then that image of ourselves gets stripped away as we pass into later adulthood. We used to take some comfort in thinking of ourselves as a son or daughter—but when our parents become ill and die, we realize that we can never go home again. We used to think of ourselves as a worker, a tradesperson or a professional in some line of work—but in retirement that self-definition gets stripped way. We used to think of ourselves as a husband, a wife, a lover, a partner—but that role is stripped from us in the anguish of our spouse's death. Eventually, we cannot even think of ourselves as a whole person, a healthy person, an independent person. We must yet again redefine ourselves. One after another, our identities are stripped away.

Nothing is quite as absolute in real life as it is implied in the above image. In real life every loss of identity is replaced by some new identity or some partial identity. For most people the "stripping away" process is not as total nor as comprehensive as we might fear. Most of us, for example, do not give up our work identities entirely. An author may still write part-time after retirement, or a minister may preach occasionally when other clerics go on vacation, or a plumber may still do odd jobs. Other people will move into less stressful roles or even part-time positions within the same general work field. These types of adjustments help us maintain our work identity at least in part while we ease our way into full retirement. Similarly, some parents find ways to continue parenting other children long after their own formal parenting is over. Grandparenting fills that need for many former parents. Others become pre-school teachers or foster parents during their own empty nest years. There are many ways to continue being a parent, maintaining that identity, even after we have lost the official role.

In spite of our partial adjustments, there are still many people who keenly feel this experience that I call "stripping away," and I suspect that to some extent we all do. It is an experience that we need to pay attention to, because like all losses in later life, it too offers us an opportunity for spiritual growth.

What is left? When all of these identities are stripped way, what do we have left? Some people feel as though they have nothing left. They do not know who they are. They despair. Much of the despair that I observe in later life may be the result of a kind of late-life identity confusion. People cannot see themselves as someone who is more than a worker or more than a child or more than a parent or more than a body. They are left with despair and hopelessness because they cannot understand themselves or value themselves apart from their former roles.

This "stripping away" process can also be an opportunity to discover a deeper understanding of ourselves, a core identity, that perhaps transcends all of our former identities. We could come to understand this process as a kind of "kenosis" or emptying of self (see Phil 2), an emptying of self of false identities in order to find a deeper, more true spiritual identity.[10] Here are a few segments from a series of conversations I had with a wonderful older gentleman whom I had asked to reflect on the process of aging in later life.

"During the last twenty years of my life I have felt somewhat like an onion. One layer after another has been stripped way from me. First my career went. Then, my beloved wife, Bea. Then, my mobility. At least I still have my writing. I do love to write, mostly little things for the local newspaper. But I expect that in time that will go. My eyes will fail or something. I wonder, sometimes, what will be left of me. What is the core of the onion really like?

"At one level it is an interesting philosophical question. What is the ultimate identity of the individual, the identity that transcends all other identities? Who are you really? Who are you at the core of your being? But it is also a very personal, very painful question for me. When each layer of the onion goes, a part of me goes. There's a lot of hurt in old age. Everything that is important to you is taken away, one by one. And this is how it is for many people in old age.

"It's a funny business, this passing through life. I say, 'That's me,' and then sometime later God takes that away, saying, 'That's not really you.' Then I say, 'Well then, that's me,' and God says, 'No, that's not you either.' That's me, but that's not me. It goes like that in life.

"The wonderful thing about this process is that each time I redefine myself I come up with a better definition. Each time I come to see myself in a more profound way. Each time I reach a little deeper into my soul. I become more of who I really am. Now, at seventy-five, I think I know myself better than I ever have in my life. I have come to see myself, I think for the first time, for what I really am. My real essence is here (points to his heart). It's not in what I did, or in my children, or in my accomplishments—no, its in what I am, in here. This is a real me (points to his heart) and it's taken me seventy-five years to get down to it.

"What a shame that we cannot help people realize what really matters sooner. We waste so many years trying to be things we are not. Then when all those things are gone, we finally realize what really matters."

This gentleman, who is a writer and a professional, is admittedly more articulate than most older adults. Yet he does seem to describe so well this process of stripping way and its potential benefits. In spite of its obvious pain, he sees some value in loss, in that it does force people to "become more of who they really are." It forces us to begin to define ourselves in deeper ways than we previously had defined ourselves. It forces us to "disidentify" with the many attachments that we have identified with over our adult years.[11] It forces us to begin to define ourselves more and more as spiritual beings.

Spiritual Identity

Most Protestant Christians are acquainted with the name Dietrich Bonhoeffer, the churchman, theologian and eventual Christian martyr who opposed Nazism in Germany. When the Nazis came to power and attempted to change historic Christian faith into a compromised "German Christianity," Bonhoeffer and his colleagues went underground, forming the "Confessing Church." Profoundly alarmed by the evils of Nazism, Bonhoeffer was led eventually to participate in a plot to assassinate Hitler. Unfortunately, the plot was discovered. He was imprisoned and eventually hanged, just a few days before the advancing Allied armies liberated the prison.

Bonhoeffer's experience in prison was not too dissimilar to what many people feel in later life in the sense that he too struggled with his loss of identity. Many of his former roles and attachments were taken from him. One of his poems, entitled "Who Am I?" and written from prison, reflects this theme. Here is a portion of that poem:

Who am I? They often tell me
I step from my cell's confinement
calmly, cheerfully, firmly,
like a squire from his country-house.
Who am I? They often tell me
I talk to my warders freely and friendly and clearly,
as though it were mine to command.
Who am I? They also tell me
I bear the days of misfortune equably, smilingly, proudly,
like one accustomed to win. . . .

Who am I? They mock me, these lonely questions of mine.
Whoever I am, thou knowest, O God, I am thine.[12]

Bonhoeffer's poem and the experience behind it illustrates the
possible positive result of the loss of identity. Such a losing might
actually help a person find a spiritual identity. As Bonhoeffer might
have described it: he does not know who he is anymore in the eyes
of others, but now, more than ever, he knows whose he is. This is
the growth opportunity that awaits us all as we lose our identity in
later life.

It seems quite clear to me that one way to prepare for the later
years of life is to cultivate a spiritual identity in the earlier years. It
is hard to form a spiritual identity in a secular world and it is hard to
form a spiritual identity during the early adult years when so much
of our lives is built around matters of this world. We cannot completely remove ourselves from the normal human attachments to career, family and health—nor should we. These relationships are
good and natural. Yet at the same time we need to remember that
these things are essentially temporary in nature. Someday they will
all pass away. A firm spiritual identity will give us a sense of "sameness and continuity" when most of our other identities are lost. A
spiritual identity can and should transcend the losses of this life.

A firm spiritual identity can also help us grieve easily and avoid
idolatry in later life. If we keep our ultimate loyalties focused on
God, we are less likely to make idols out of lost loved objects, however prized those attachments might have been. Trust in a God who
transcends all losses is the bulwark against the temptation to make

any single object into a god. Or to put differently, if our primary identity is spiritual, we are better able to resist the temptation to make any one of our earthly identities ultimate. A firm spiritual identity, therefore, can help us grieve our losses, because we know that all lost attachments, no matter how cherished, are not matters of life and death. We can let go. We can trust. We can grieve easily—even joyfully—because our identity is rooted deep in a spiritual soil that transcends the losses of the life cycle.

Life in the later years is essentially a spiritual journey precisely because the loss process forces us more and more to focus on and value our spiritual selves.[13] There is, therefore, great potential for spiritual growth and renewal in and through the loss of identity.

Notes

1. Erik H. Erikson, *Identity, Youth and Crisis* (New York: W.W. Norton and Co., 1968), p. 19.

2. See Allen Wheelis, *The Quest for Identity* (New York: W.W. Norton, 1978) or David Riesman, *The Lonely Crowd* (New Haven: Yale University Press, 1961).

3. *Diagnostic and Statistical Manual of Mental Disorders*, Third Edition (Washington: American Psychiatric Association, 1980), p. 65.

4. This point is clearest in his recent writings, where he sees every crisis as relived or foreshadowed in each stage of the life cycle. See Erik H. Erikson, Joan M. Erikson and Helen Q. Kivnick, *Vital Involvement in Old Age*.

5. For example, see Eda LeShan, *The Wonderful Crisis of Middle Age* (New York: Warner Books, 1973).

6. For example, see Lynne Caine's *Widow* or chapter seven of Colin Murray Parkes' *Bereavement*.

7. Younger people can also benefit greatly from friendships with older adults. Such friendships help prepare younger people for the issues and trials of old age. Perhaps one reason why so many of us modern people have trouble with aging is that we have isolated ourselves from older people and thereby robbed ourselves of the opportunity to prepare ourselves.

8. There are many theories of what constitutes successful aging. I am largely supporting a viewpoint that argues that personality factors are the most influential variables. This theory is associated with the name Bernice L. Neugarten. See *Personality in Middle and Late Life: Empirical Studies* (New York: Atherton, 1964) or *Middle Age and Aging.*

9. See Robert C. Peck, "Psychological Developments in the Second Half of Life," in Bernice L. Neugarten, editor, *Middle Age and Aging*, pp. 88–92.

10. Evelyn Eaton Whitehead has used this image as one of the religious images for aging. See "Religious Images of Aging: An Examination of Themes in Contemporary Christian Thought," in Carol LeFevre and Perry LeFevre, *Aging and the Human Spirit*, pp. 56–67.

11. Psychosynthesis, a form of psychotherapy, actually has a technique called "Disidentification," in which a client says, "I am my work . . . I am not my work. I am a parent . . . I am not a parent," and so on. This technique is supposed to help a person discover a deeper sense of self, a self that transcends roles and attachments. See Roberto Assagioli, *Psychosynthesis: A Manual of Principles and Techniques* (New York: Hobbes, Dorman and Co., 1965).

12. Dietrich Bonheoffer, *Letters and Papers From Prison*, Revised Edition, Edited by Eberhard Bethge (New York: Macmillan, 1967), pp. 188–89.

13. There is considerable debate in the literature on aging regarding the role of religion and religious sentiment in later life. The debate centers on whether people become more religious in later life or not. I am taking the position that people can and do become more religious in later life, not because of any innate tendency or even fear of death, but because the losses of later life strip away most of our other identities, forcing us to look inward.

Chapter 10

Faith and the Art of Suffering

"For whoever would save his life will lose it, and whoever loses his life for my sake will find it" (Mat 16:25).

We have completed our survey of the major losses in the later years of life. We have described some of the unique features of each loss. As was noted at the start of this book, these losses have not been presented in any chronological order. In fact these losses are as much themes in later life as they are specific loss events. They are both events and processes. The loss of parents, for example, is associated with a specific event, their deaths, but this loss can also be experienced as process as they decline in health. Losses like the loss of health or identity are certainly processes, but even here it is sometimes specific events, marker events, that crystallize our feelings of loss.

Given the pervasive presence and power of losses in later life, we now ask the question in this final chapter: How can we age well? Why do some people cope easily with the losses of later life while others seem to deteriorate mentally, spiritually and physically? What are the ingredients that make one age well? Put on your theological caps and think with me for a moment about the nature of life in the later years, about human faith and about God's grace in our lives.

The Final Loss

Up to this point in the book, there is one major loss in later life that we have not talked about directly. This is the loss of our own life (which can also be experienced as both event and process). I have chosen not to deal with our own death as a loss for several reasons. Chiefly, our own death is not a developmental loss in the normal sense of the word. Our own death is not a loss that we experience after-the-fact—at least not in this life. Its influence on our lives is entirely anticipatory.

Yet in another sense, of course, our personal demise is the ultimate loss. It is the loss that stands behind—or, should I say, ahead of—all other losses. It is the loss that colors and influences every loss. It is the loss that makes all of us anxious, an anxiety that becomes the very background music to life itself. Every loss of the life cycle foreshadows the loss of life itself. In a sense then we do live through this loss of life. We live through it every time we lose anyone or anything we love.

Some people have suggested that the fear of death is really a young person's problem. People who live many years, many long years, do not fear death as much as people in the prime of life. As death comes close, many people make peace with "the enemy." They anticipate it. They do their grief work in advance, and in many cases, especially when physical pain has been severe, death comes as a relief, as a welcomed friend. I am not convinced that this adage is universally true. Yet it is true enough that it should give us cause to reflect on its dynamic.

One of the reasons why death is not always feared as much among older people as it is among younger people has to do with the fact that most older people have lived through many small deaths. Death is nothing new to them. They have experienced many "deaths" in the course of their lifetimes. Hopefully they also have experienced many resurrections. Perhaps they have discovered that new life does emerge out of the ashes of the old. If they have been fortunate enough to experience this dying and rising process once, even several times, then they are prepared for their ultimate trial. Such people can and do approach their own deaths with a kind of experiental confidence that comes only from having lived through many other small deaths and resurrections.

Mabel was an eighty-three year old retired Christian missionary with whom I had a delightful conversation about her life and approaching death. She often told me in her later years that she did not fear death, but neither did she boast of such assurance as many Christians do. Her attitude toward her own death was just a quiet confidence, a confidence that fascinated me greatly. On one occasion I pursued the theme with her.

"Death has become my friend," she noted, "an ever-present companion in my old age. I guess you get used to it—death. I don't fear it as much as I used to. It will come to me in good time, no sooner, no later."

"What has enabled you to overcome the fear?" I asked.

"I don't know that I have entirely. It's still alarming when I get sick. But I think I now fear the pain of dying more than death itself. . . . I have more faith in God than I used to. Isn't it really a fear of the unknown? Isn't that all it is—just the unknown? If so, then I have faced the unknown before many times."

"Describe for me one of those times when you faced the unknown," I continued.

"The one that I recall most was when Christopher and I first went out to the mission field. That was a real unknown! We didn't have any idea of what was going to happen to us; we just knew that this was something we had to do. I was pregnant at the time with Martha, and little Timothy was three years old. Surely, part of me didn't want to leave our church in Maryland. It was comfortable. It was a fine congregation. We were surrounded by many loving people there."

"They were not easy years," she continued, "those years in the mission field. Not easy at all. One time Chris got sick with malaria, and there I was in a strange country with two young children, no means of support, and a sick, possibly dying husband."

"Those were your darkest hours?" I asked. "What did you do?"

"I don't remember exactly. I think I just sat down and cried. It's funny, though, because now when I look back on those years, I think of them as the very best years of our lives. We made wonderful friends during that time, people who still call us and write us. Last year one of the young girls from one of our mission families, came to this country for college. She stopped to see us. Too bad Christopher was not here anymore to see her. She is so grown up, so mature."

"New life came out of a situation that initially you thought would be a disaster," I observed.

"I guess that's why I don't fear death as much. God stayed with us, with Chris and me during those times, and they turned into the best of times. I really believe that 'In all things God works for good for those who love him.' I know this to be true in my life, and that's what takes the edge off of death for me. . . . But it wasn't easy. Those were rough times."

"God transformed your darkness into light, your worst times into the best times, your death into new life."

"Yes, indeed," she concluded.

Many of the transitions of life, like that of Mabel's relocation to the mission field, involve mini-death experiences. In this case it was the death of a life style in Maryland. In other situations someone may have literally died—a spouse, a parent, a home that is left behind. In other cases a role has died. We are no longer a parent or a son or daughter or an executive. In almost all cases some part of us, some piece of our worth or identity, has died. Maybe our worth has been diminished because we no longer work. Maybe our good health has vanished. Perhaps our appearance has faded. Each and every loss event that I have described in this book carries with it a type of death, and every death brings with it grief and sorrow.

We need to grieve these many "deaths" if we expect to pass through these loss experiences. We cannot hold back or get side-tracked in idolatry. We must enter fully into our pain and suffering. We must also enter into the fear—the fear of the unknown future, as Mabel put it—that comes with every loss event. If we grieve well, then in time we do come to the other side of sorrow. We do recapture our emotional energies and begin again to invest ourselves into new loves, new identities, new attachments. In the process of doing all this, we discover something very amazing. We discover that we are different than we were before the loss. We are now new persons. We have been changed, even transformed by the very process of grieving itself. We have passed over into a new stage of our lives, and with that passage we have taken on a new role, a new identity, new priorities and new relationships. New life has emerged out of loss.

Learning To Suffer Well

For Christians Jesus is the model and example that we seek to imitate. Perhaps by looking at how Jesus coped with his suffering and eventual death, as in the story of the garden of Gethsemane,[1] we might identify a few clues regarding how we can learn to suffer well. In fact, the passion, death and eventual resurrection of Jesus Christ can be understood as a paradigm for how we are to deal with loss, sorrow and faith in later life.

If we view Jesus' death and resurrection as a unified process, we immediately notice the importance of the sequential order of the events. Jesus had to die in order to live. He could not do the reverse: be glorified now and suffer later. He had to lose in order to gain. That is the necessary order of events. In a similar way we face the same succession of events every time we face a loss in later life. We lose . . . we suffer . . . then we find new life. We might wish to reverse the order. Denial is a way of trying to reverse the order of these events, trying to avoid loss, trying to "let the cup pass." If we do attempt to avoid grieving, we truncate the normal sequential order, and end up "losing life" (see Mat 16:25). What a strange paradox!

Indeed, there is something about life, particularly life in the later years, that suggests that at times we must lose in order to gain. We must let go in order to find. We must let go of something old in order to receive something new. When losses emerge in our lives, our first impulse is not to let go, but to save, to control, to cling. Yet, it is precisely by doing so that we cut ourselves off from life. Only by losing, by grieving, by letting go, will we find new life. It is indeed a paradox.

Suffering then becomes a necessary part of the death and resurrection experience. Jesus' passion was not shallow, nor mild, nor tempered by the sure knowledge of the glory that awaited him. No, his suffering, his fear, and his agony were real, as real as any of our worst sufferings. He endured a *real* human death.[2] He died a death like ours. The gospel writers and the early church writers were very clear on this point.

Similarly, our suffering is a necessary part of our dying and rising. We cannot find new life unless we are willing to enter into our suffering. For us that suffering means grieving. We cannot move on to a new life stage unless we grieve, fully and completely. Grieving is emotional suffering. It is the necessary suffering that allows us to let go of the past. It is the emotional process that gradually enables us to withdraw our energy from that which is now dead. Obviously, if we cannot do this, we cannot live again.

In a modern culture that promotes instant gratification in every commercial and cultivates the pleasures of the flesh as a birthright, it is little wonder that we have lost the art of suffering. We do not suffer well—and, in large measure, we do not grieve well. The two statements are connected. In both cases the culture encourages us to medicate pain, to mask negative feelings, and to flee from sorrow, rather than to enter into it. Yet, the message of the gospel is clear enough: we must embrace sufferings if we hope to transcend our losses.

The question might legitimately be asked then, "How are we able to embrace suffering?" Suffering hurts. Grief hurts. What enables us to suffer well?

The garden of Gethsemane story tells us very directly that Jesus was frightened, that Jesus did not want to die, that Jesus was suffering, but that he chose to obey the will of "the heavenly Father." Clearly, he had a faith that sustained him and strengthened him in spite of his fears, his doubts and the pain he was experiencing.[3] Faith sustained Jesus and somehow enabled him to enter into his loss and eventually transcend it.

Faith as Trust and Belief

If grieving is so painful and yet so important for us, how do we enter into it? What helps us grieve? What enables us to suffer well? I am suggesting that faith plays a major, critical role in facilitating the grieving process and thereby birthing new life within us. In order to convince you of this point, however, I need to explain to you what I mean by faith.

Simply put, faith is the human response to the Ultimate. For me, faith has two interrelated and indispensable dimensions: trust and belief. We trust in God and we believe in God. The two are separate aspects of faith, but essentially inseparable.[4] Each dimension of faith, trust and belief helps us grieve.

Faith as trust refers to our trusting attitude toward God. It is largely an attitude, a pre-cognitive stance toward God, in fact toward life in general.[5] We do not think our way into trusting. It is more automatic, more feeling oriented and in fact more universal than thinking would allow. Every human needs to and in fact does trust in something beyond himself or herself. It is human to trust. Faith as trust manifests itself as a trusting attitude toward life, toward others, toward oneself, toward the providential events of life. Faith as trust allows us to enter into life in all of its fullness with an experiental confidence that "it is good" (Gen 1:25,31). However this trusting attitude alone is not sufficient. Trust needs to be trust *in* something. We cannot trust in a vacuum.

Faith also has a belief dimension. Faith must be faith in something. The something could be our spouse, our company, the U.S. government, materialism, or, better yet, God. This is the cognitive dimension of faith. These are the things we believe, we examine, we assent to as doctrine. We do not feel these things, but we believe them. We think them. Faith as belief is also the particular aspect of faith. We have faith in a particular object, a particular set of beliefs or a particular religion. Each person's particular beliefs will vary widely. For faith as belief to be most helpful, our belief must be in something larger than ourselves, and the larger the better. Beliefs that transcend the moment, the individual and the temporal are most enduring and the most helpful in times of loss.

Obviously faith as trust and faith as belief are two sides of the same coin. Each dimension needs the other in order to be complete. It is impossible to trust in the abstract. We always trust in something particular. Likewise, it is impossible to believe in something particular without some sort of personal response on our part. Belief is not truly belief without commitment. Similarly, we cannot just feel our way to faith. We must also think our way to faith. Both dimensions, faith as feeling and faith as thinking, make up the whole person and the whole response to God.

The Role of Faith in Grieving

When we experience a loss event or first become aware of a loss process, we face an existential choice. It is largely an unconscious choice, but it is a crucial turning point in our mental/spiritual growth. It is the choice between grieving and avoiding grief. There is a powerful temptation in us humans to avoid pain. Yet, there is also a strong urge to face it, to let go and to cry. The forces of avoidance and the forces of growth vie to determine our "decision." One critical factor in tipping the scale in the direction of growth is the individual's faith. If a man can trust the grief process and believe that there is meaning beyond all this agony, then he can more easily grieve. And, conversely, if a woman has little trust and few enduring beliefs, then she will find it more difficult to grieve. Faith as trust is one factor in facilitating a person's ability to grieve.

Benjamin couldn't cry. His mother was dying of cancer in a nearby nursing home—a slow, lingering, prolonged dying. He couldn't sleep at night. He was nervous all day. He couldn't concentrate on his work. He sought me out for advice. Benjamin was very close to his mother. She had been his confidante, friend and motivator even well into his adult years. Her death would be a major loss/change in his life. With my prodding, Benjamin would get close to tears. His eyes would water up. His lip would quiver some—but he couldn't let go. "Come on, Ben," I would urge him. "Let it out. Let it go. I know your pain is great."

"It's too difficult, doctor. I'm afraid to break down in front of people. I know I need to cry, but it's not my style. That's one of the things my mother always told us kids, you know. Don't show people your emotions, don't show them where you're vulnerable."

"It's a real double bind for you, then," I said. "You want to cry over your mother's imminent death; you love her very much; but you are also bound by her instructions not to cry over her. It would be showing disloyalty to her to cry over her?"

"Emotions are troublesome in our family. It goes back to when my people were slaves. You didn't show the white man your weaknesses. They'd get you in trouble. My mother knows I love her. I don't need to cry over her now to prove anything."

"But you're hurting, Ben, and when we hurt, it's often helpful to cry," I observed.

"As I said, emotions are troublesome. They get out of control, overwhelm you with passion or anguish. I prefer to stay in charge of my emotions. It's safer that way."

"I hope that when and where you do feel safe, you might relax and allow yourself some grief, expressed and shared in your own way. I think you will feel a whole lot better."

Benjamin's mother died within a few days of this conversation, and he went through the funeral largely self-controlled. I suspect that he let down some in private, but he certainly did not enter into the process. And he continued to be bothered by physical symptoms for months after his mother's death. Benjamin had a "choice" between allowing himself tears or holding them back. It was not entirely a free choice. There were cultural and family issues that limited his freedom to respond in some way other than a controlled manner. Perhaps if Benjamin had had a more prolonged therapeutic relationship, one in which he could come to feel safe, he might have shared more of his pain. Unfortunately, that option was not available to us.

The choice is whether to cry or not. It is as simple and as universal as all that. Each time we deal with a loss, we "face a choice," says Paul Tournier, "a choice between facing reality and evasion."[6] We encounter the same choice over and over again. On the surface it is a choice between whether to grieve or not, but at a deeper level it is a choice whether to grow or not. Surely there are gender and cultural factors that influence how freely we grieve. There is also a trust factor, a faith factor. If we can trust, we can more freely enter into our grief. Without this trust, we cling to control.

What of faith as belief? How does faith as belief, specifically faith in God, help this process? Belief in a God who transcends the human life cycle and all of our losses can sustain us in times of sorrow. Further, belief in a God whose love for us is constant, dependable and trustworthy is important in a time when it feels as though life is very unpredictable, untrustable. Frequently the grief process includes periods of emotional confusion, pain and loneliness. We do not feel close to God at times in the grief process. These can be terrible times, dark nights of the soul. In these moments, we can still hope because our eyes are set on something beyond the moment. In these moments we do not *feel* our faith, but we can still *think* it.

Marge was a very devout Catholic woman, but when her husband died at the young age of forty-six, leaving her with three almost grown children, she was devastated. She could not believe that God would have allowed this to happen. It was a total, shocking break with her previous experience of God and faith. By her own telling she had always enjoyed a close relationship with her church and God. Now, amidst her sorrow, however, she felt lost, alone, as though God had abandoned her.

"At night after the children are in bed, I sit down and talk with God, just the way I have since I was a young child myself. But now, God doesn't seem to talk back. I pray and pray, but there's nothing— just silence."

"What do you want God to tell you," the priest asked.

"I want an answer. I want to know why this has happened to me. What is the purpose of Charles' death. No, what I really want is just to not feel alone, to know God is still beside me."

"How do you know God is not with you?" he continued.

"I don't feel him here. There's nothing here in my heart, just emptiness and darkness and pain." She cries as she adds, "I'm so alone."

"Think with me for a moment, Marge. I know you feel very alone right now. Do you think that God stops loving us just because we do not feel it? Do you think God is no longer with you just because he doesn't speak for a while. You know that God is always here. You just don't happen to feel it right now."

"I understand what you mean, Father, but it is hard. It's hard believing God is with me when all I feel is pain. It's hard to believe in God right now."

"Yes, I know. You are a very feeling person, but for the time being we're going to have to rely on the thinking part of your faith. *Think* that there will be something beyond the darkness, something beyond the pain. We do not know exactly what it will be yet—nobody does—but we know there will be something good. I guess what I am talking about is hope.

"Right now, all I have is hope . . . and pain."

Humans are both minds and bodies. Faith has both a body dimension, manifested as feelings, and a mental dimension, manifested through our mind. When we are overwhelmed by our feelings, as in deep sorrow, then we must rely on our minds, our beliefs to sustain us. Hope is believing even when we don't feel trusting. Hope is in things "unseen" (Rom 8:24-25). If we could see the good future, then it would be easy to trust, to have faith. In the times when we cannot see anything good, we rely solely on faith as belief.[7]

In a culture that has become increasingly dominated by the ethos and norms of psychology, it is hard for people to rely on faith as belief. The criteria for faith becomes whether or not we feel it. We expect to feel close to God, and if we do not, then surely God must not be there. We have a hard time understanding that something could be true, even though we do not feel it. This assumption also causes problems with many marriages, when an overly romantic spouse says, "I love you, but I'm not in love." He or she fails to see a kind of love that is larger than feelings, a love that can sustain a relationship even when one does not momentarily feel "in love." Similarly, in times of sorrow, we need a faith as belief to sustain us when we momentarily do not feel God's presence.

So the two dimensions of faith, trust and belief, each has a role to play in helping us grieve and thereby helping us grow. Faith as trust encourages us to trust our feelings, to let go emotionally and trust the process nature of grief itself. And faith as belief sustains and supports us as we are going through this valley of sorrow. It gives us hope when there appears to be none. Trust helps us let go; beliefs sustain us. Release and structure. Pain and comfort. Each aspect of grieving is important, as is each dimension of faith.

Faith Has a History

We do not have faith in a vacuum nor do we create faith in the crisis of the moment. Our experience of faith has a history—a history that influences how we respond to the loss currently before us. If we have responded with faith in times of loss in the past, then we are more likely to have experienced growth and new life in and through our sorrow. Thus, when the next loss comes our way, we are more likely to respond with faith again.[8]

"Sometimes I look back on my life, and think 'This isn't so bad.' I thought it would be horrible, living without the children and

Chuck. I didn't know what I was going to do with myself when the kids grew up. In fact, I was secretly dreading it. Then the marriage dissolved too—that was the clincher! Now I had to grow up."

"What have you learned, then, from all of this?" the counselor asked.

"I like my life now. I am a better person now than I was before, no question, and I am becoming even stronger. And I love my career. All this would not have happened if I had clung to that motherhood stuff. I guess in some ways that's what killed the marriage and almost killed me too. I wasn't a person then, and I wasn't going to become one until I was forced to give it up, give all of it up."

"And God?" the counselor queried. "Where was God in this process for you?"

"I think God was pushing me toward new life. I now think that he had been doing this for years, but I didn't have the eyes to see it. I think I have a stronger faith now because of what I went through. When you pass through the River Jordan and see that there is another side, your faith is strengthened."

"Perhaps in the future you will not find the next transition so hard," the counselor concluded.

The opposite dynamic is equally true and equally possible. In times of loss some people have little faith, either as trust or as belief, to rely on. They are afraid to grieve. They are afraid of their emotions—the sorrow and the fear. They find grieving to be very difficult at best. And they have few beliefs to sustain them in the dark days of hopelessness. They have no hope in a future they cannot see, and so they cling to the past. As a result of all this, they do not experience new life. They muddle through grief at best and move into the next stage of life, carrying behind them a string of unresolved sorrows.

Humans are never completely predictable of course, and faith never exists in the absolute. Throughout our life cycle, faith and fear are in constant interplay. My point is only that as we approach the later years of life with their culminating loss experiences, each of us brings our own personal faith history to bear upon the current crisis. This current loss is linked emotionally to all other losses in our life. Our "decision" to grieve or not to grieve is based in part on the character of our previous experience with grief, sorrow and faith.

Faith Is Relational

Faith is not experienced in isolation. We are all relational creatures, and our faith is either supported or undermined by our closest relationships. Others who have faith when we do not can facilitate our faith. In a real sense we borrow their faith for a while. The importance of others is especially crucial in matters of loss, when our normally adequate faith might feel very inadequate. Loved ones, who have faith, can facilitate our grieving even if our faith is momentarily shaky. These loved ones, however, have to be willing to be engaged with us in our sorrow and theirs.

The movie "Ordinary People," based on the novel by Judith Guest, is a wonderful study in abnormal grief and the critical role of others in facilitating or blocking grief.[9] As you will recall, Conrad is the second of two teenage sons born to his well-to-do parents, Calvin and Beth. The oldest son Buck, who was successful at almost every thing he did and who appears to be his parents' favorite, died in a boating accident. Conrad was also involved in the boating accident, but managed to survive. Soon thereafter Conrad attempted suicide and is briefly hospitalized. Conrad still cannot grieve, however, and is haunted by flashbacks and nightmares. He also shows a lack of appetite, preoccupation, irritability and of course continuing depression—all of which are the classic symptoms of a stuck grief process. As we get a fuller picture of what this family has gone through in the death of Buck, we are struck with how little they talk of Buck, the accident, or, for that matter, anything meaningful. Conrad complains, "We don't connect." What becomes clear is that the whole family, particularly Conrad's mother Beth, is denying the loss, refusing to grieve and trying wherever possible to "escape" from the scene both emotionally and physically. Conrad needs to grieve, but he has no social support for it.

Conrad gets into regular therapy with Dr. Berger, a local psychiatrist, who helps him begin to feel again. Here we see Conrad struggling with his own inner war between denial and grieving. Part of him wants to feel again and part of him flees from the tremendous pain therein. In one particularly powerful scene, Conrad has just learned that a friend from the hospital has killed herself, news that throws him into an emotional upheaval and places him on the edge of attempting to take his own life again. During the emergency session with his therapist, the conversation goes something like this.

"Feelings are scary," says Dr. Berger. "Sometimes they're painful. If you can't feel pain, you are not going to feel anything else either. You're alive, and don't tell me you don't feel that."

"It doesn't feel good," responds Conrad.

"It is good—believe me," Berger affirms.

"How do you know?" the boy asks.

"Because I'm your friend."

"I don't know what I would have done if you hadn't been here," says Conrad. "Are you really my friend?"

"I am. Count on it."

In that instant Conrad lets go, embraces his new-found friend and weeps deeply. This is the grief that Conrad had held back for these many months. This is the pain that never came out at the funeral, the pain that was turned inward as depression and self-hate.

Faith has a relational component. Conrad had little faith in part because his parents had little faith. He could not trust his feelings. There was an implicit operational belief that "negative feelings are bad." Pain was to be avoided, not worked through. Yet through his friend's trust and support, Conrad entered into that scary world of feelings. He entered into his pain for the first time. Then, and only then, did he begin to get well. In that instant, Conrad was aware of the existential choice, to let go or to control. Unlike previous moments, where he chose control, this time the presence of a friend who had faith enables him to grieve.

Idolatry and Avoiding Grief

Some people have little faith, and as a result they do not grieve easily. If that was all there was to it, enough would be said. However, humans are meaning-making animals. We have an innate desire and capacity for faith. In this sense faith is, as James W. Fowler has suggested, universal in all humans.[10] Paul Tillich, the great Protestant theologian of the mid-twentieth century, used to make the same point. He argued that all humans had their ultimate concerns. It did not matter so much whether one was Catholic, Presbyterian, Muslim or even agnostic. Everyone had a faith. The content of that faith can vary widely, but the structure of faith was universal. If a person's faith in God is too little or too fragile or even non-existent, then he or she places faith in other objects, relationships or meanings. People need faith, and in the absence of traditional objects of faith they will seek to lodge their faith elsewhere.

Going back to the movie for a moment, consider now Conrad's mother Beth who is an example of someone who "chose" not to grieve. Her style was to avoid pain and strive to cover up anything messy or unpleasant. Besides the obvious damage that this "decision" did to Conrad and eventually to her marriage, focus just on her functioning. Do you see anything familiar? She cannot love. She cannot give. She is emotionally aloof. Her interest is in keeping life orderly, pleasant and pretty. The house must be clean. No one must know about our family secrets. She refuses to allow a pet dog (which would be both messy and giving). She is unable to return love, even when Conrad gets healed enough to embrace her. Gradually we see how empty her life really is. We see clearly that she is choosing "to save her life" and is therefore ending up "losing her life."

I would argue that if we look at this "living human document" theologically, we would see a woman caught in idolatry. Beth has little faith in God or in anything else that could have encouraged her grief or sustained her in sorrow. Not trusting in this God, she flees from her pain. But where else did she put her faith? What becomes her god? She creates an idol called control, and as long as she worships at this altar it gives her happiness (of sorts). Control becomes her *raison d'être*, her identity and her value system. What becomes increasingly clear to her husband is that she cannot change. She is trapped, imprisoned, maybe even a slave. She ceased to grow spiritually when she refused to grieve.

In the absence of genuine faith, we humans do tend to create our own idols—idols that become particularly potent in times of loss, idols that enslave us and block us from grieving and thereby growing into new life.

Successful Aging

In the literature on aging there is considerable attention given to the topic of successful aging. It continues to fascinate researchers who study the psychology of aging, why most people seem to decline mentally, psychologically and socially in the later years of life, while others, admittedly the minority, seem to grow and expand mentally, psychologically and socially sometimes right up to the point of their deaths. Various researchers have attempted to describe what they consider to be optimum aging.[11] Of course, everyone ages slightly differently, but in general what are the characteristics of personality or behavior that enable one to age well, in full mental and spiritual health? It is indeed an interesting question, one that is not only at the heart of gerontology, but at the heart of the meaning of life itself. In this final chapter, I have offered a modest and brief contribution to that discussion by suggesting that faith plays a key role in enabling successful aging.

Since losses are so much of a part of life in the later years, people who wish to age successfully need to be able to deal with losses successfully. They must be able to grieve easily and completely. They must be able to suffer well. That is easier said than done. Most people don't seem to grieve easily or completely, an observation which I think accounts for why there is so much mental, psychological and social decline in later life. Most older people are just overwhelmed by the cumulative nature of loss in later life and eventually "give up" in despair.

Yet, there are some people, rare people, who seem to suffer well, who seem to rebound from one loss after another. They do not have fewer troubles than the rest of us. No, they have their share of sufferings, maybe even more than most, but they still seem to appreciate life and look forward to living. They seem to have a deep acceptance of life or faith in life's goodness that sustains them and carries them through all of life's sorrows. According to Erikson and others, most of us do not acquire, if we ever do, this acceptance of life until late in life.[12] Maybe these few rare people who seem to age so well have learned acceptance much sooner than the rest of us. Maybe they are what Erikson called *homo religiosus*, people who have made "the integrity crisis . . . a lifelong and chronic crisis."[13]

Because of this deep acceptance of the inevitability of loss, persons who age successfully have the ability to suffer well.[14] They accept the inevitability of loss in later life. They know that they have no choice about that. But they do know that they have a choice about how they shall respond to loss. They choose to cry, they choose to suffer deeply, and they also choose to love again . . . and again . . . and again. It is as if they continue to believe that "life is good" no matter how tragic or painful life becomes at times. As a result they continue to care. They continue to grow. They continue to rise above their sufferings. They continue to go forth joyfully.

All this is made possible, in part, because of their faith. Through faith, their losses have been transformed into transitions, new life has emerged out of old, resurrection has followed death. Thus these rare people now come to the end of their lives with a measure of assurance that the same God who brought them through all of life's previous losses will also walk with them through this final loss, together into the world beyond.

Notes

1. I have always been curious how and why this story of the garden of Gethsemane, particularly Jesus' private conversations with God, got preserved as Sacred Scripture. There is something very important about our knowing that Jesus was frightened and doubtful and how he dealt with these doubts and feelings.

2. Historically, the heresy that argued that Christ was not really human, but only appeared to be human, is called docetism. The gospel stories about Jesus' passion and dying indicate how strongly the early Christians opposed this point of view and saw Jesus' humanity as central to his identity and mission.

3. Faith could thus be understood as a type of courage or as resulting in courage. For a discussion of faith as courage, see Paul Tillich's *Dynamics of Faith* (New York: Harper and Row, 1957).

4. This distinction was first introduced to me by reading Rudolf Bultmann's *Theology of the New Testament,* vol. 1 (New York: Scribner's Sons, 1951), pp. 314–24, where Bultmann argues that Paul's understanding of faith included both an obedience dimension and a

belief dimension. James W. Fowler has also referred to this distinction between faith as trust and faith as belief in his *Stages of Faith* (New York: Harper and Row, 1981), a distinction that he drew from Wilfred Cantwell Smith's *Faith and Belief* (Princeton: Princeton University Press, 1979).

5. Faith as trust is very close to what Erik Erikson means by "basic trust." For a fuller discussion of this point, see chapter 9 in my *Grief and Growth* (Mahwah, New Jersey: Paulist Press, 1985), pp. 192–215.

6. Paul Tournier, *Learning To Grow Old,* pp. 184–85.

7. Erik Erikson also linked faith, in the form of basic trust, and hope. He suggested that "hope is the ontogenetic basis for faith." See *Insight and Responsibility* (New York: Norton, 1964), p. 118. I am suggesting the reverse priority—that faith makes hope possible.

8. Several writers, particularly James W. Fowler, have suggested that faith has a history and in fact changes shape and content over the life cycle. My view puts the emphasis on how faith, particularly as trust, remains the same over the life span. Erik Erikson has suggested that the initial developmental crisis, basic trust vs. basic mistrust, while resolved initially in infancy, does continue to be a theme in every developmental crisis, especially, I would suggest, during developmental crises that involve loss experiences.

9. It is interesting to note that James W. Fowler also quotes this story, from the book version, in his book *Stages of Faith*. We are making different points, but he seems to sense, as I do, that this story is about faith as much as it is about grief. In fact I would suggest that faith and grief are deeply and intricately connected. One cannot grieve well without an implicit faith.

10. James W. Fowler *Stages of Faith,* pp. 4–5.

11. For example, see Richard H. Williams and Claudine G. Wirth, *Lives Through the Years: Styles of Life and Successful Aging* (New York: Atherton Press, 1965).

12. In describing the last developmental crisis of the life cycle, ego integrity vs. despair, Erikson defines integrity in this way: "It is the *acceptance* of one's one and only life cycle as something that had to be and that, by necessity, permitted of no substitutions . . . " (emphasis is mine) in *Childhood and Society,* p. 268. It is also interesting to note that Elisabeth Kübler-Ross labeled the last stage of the emo-

tional process of terminally ill patients "acceptance." Like Erikson, she contrasted acceptance with resignation. Acceptance was more of a positive embracing of life, accepting of loss and what has to be.

13. Erik H. Erikson *Young Man Luther* (New York: W.W. Norton, 1958), p. 261.

14. It is interesting to note that the ability to suffer, usually termed "long suffering" in Scripture, is often listed as one of the results of having faith.

Further Reading
(A Selected Bibliography)

There are many books on aging and grief worth reading. I have tried to select books here that are readable and scholarly and written from an integrated perspective.

Baum, Gregory, editor. *Work and Religion*. New York: Seabury Press, 1980.

Becker, Arthur H. *Ministry with Older Persons: A Guide for Clergy and Congregations*. Minneapolis: Augsburg Publishing House, 1986.

Bianchi, Eugene C. *Aging as a Spiritual Journey*. New York: Crossroad, 1982.

Browning, Don S. *Generative Man: Psychoanalytic Perspectives*. Philadelphia: Westminster Press, 1973.

Capps, Donald. *Life Cycle Theory and Pastoral Care*. Philadelphia: Fortress Press, 1983.

Clements, William M. *Care and Counseling of the Aging*. Philadelphia: Fortress Press, 1979.

————, editor. *Ministry with the Aging: Design, Challenges, Foundations*. New York: Harper and Row, 1981.

Faber, Heije. *Striking Sails: A Pastoral-Psychological View of Growing Older in Our Society*. translated by Kenneth R. Mitchell. Nashville: Abingdon Press, 1984.

Fowler, James W. *Stages of Faith*. New York: Harper and Row, 1981.

Hulme, William E. *Vintage Years: Growing Older with Meaning and Hope*. Philadelphia: Westminster Press, 1986.

Lapsley, James H. *Salvation and Health: The Interlocking Processes of Life*. Philadelphia: Westminster Press, 1972.

LeFevre, Carol and Perry LeFevre. *Aging and the Human Spirit: A Reader in Religion and Gerontology*. second edition. Chicago: Exploration Press, 1981.

Lester, Andrew D. and Judith L. Lester. *Understanding Aging Parents*. Philadelphia: Westminster Press, 1980.

Maitland, David J. *Looking Both Ways: A Theology for Midlife*. Atlanta: John Knox Press, 1985.

McClellan, Robert W. *Claiming the Frontier: Ministry and Older People*. Los Angeles: University of Southern California Press, 1977.

Mitchell, Kenneth R. and Herbert Anderson. *All Our Losses, All Our Griefs: Resources for Pastoral Care*. Philadelphia: Westminster Press, 1983.

Nouwen, Henri J.M. and Walter J. Gaffney. *Aging: The Fulfillment of Life*. Garden City, N.Y.: Image Books, 1976.

Robb, Thomas Bradley. *The Bonus Years: Foundations for Ministry with Older Persons*. Valley Forge: The Judson Press, 1968.

Soelle, Dorothee. with Shirley A. Cloyes. *To Work and To Love: A Theology of Creation*. Philadelphia: Fortress Press, 1984.

Sullender, R. Scott. *Grief and Growth: Pastoral Resources for Emotional and Spiritual Growth*. Mahwah, New Jersey: Paulist Press, 1985.

Tournier, Paul. *Learn To Grow Old*. New York: Harper, 1972.